Ron Rood's

VERMONT

A Nature Guide

Ron Rood's

VERMONT

A Nature Guide

by
Ronald Rood

Illustrated by Reed A. Prescott III

The New England Press
Shelburne, Vermont

For additional copies of this book or for a catalog
of our other New England and nature titles, please write:

The New England Press
P.O. Box 575
Shelburne, Vermont 05482

ILLUSTRATOR'S ACKNOWLEDGMENTS

I would like to thank the authors and publishers of the following books
for providing models for some of my drawings:

La Rue, Leonard III. *How I Photograph Wildlife and Nature.* New York:
W. W. Norton, 1984.

Rand, Austin L. *American Water and Game Birds.* New York: E. P. Dutton
& Co., 1956.

Terres, John K. *The Audubon Society Encyclopedia of North American Birds.*
New York: Alfred A. Knopf, 1980.

In addition, I'd like to thank Bob and Lorraine Patterson, whose broken
garage window supplied me with a wayward grouse.

Rood, Ronald N.
   Ron Rood's Vermont : a nature guide / by Ronald Rood ;
illustrations by Reed A. Prescott III. — 1st ed.
      p.   cm.
   Bibliography: p.
   Includes index.
   ISBN 0-933050-56-9 : $10.95
   1. Natural history—Vermont—Guide-books. I. Title. II. Title:
Vermont.
QH105.V7R63 1988
508.743—dc19   88-9856
                                                         CIP

Maps by Erich Glenn Griesser.
All maps should be used in conjunction with one of the maps or atlases
mentioned on pages 203–5.

It's with gratitude for having shared his knowledge and experiences with us that the artist and author respectfully dedicate this book to the memory of our friend and neighbor,

M. DORAN PIERCE

Oh Lord, how many are Thy works!
In wisdom Thou hast made them all;
The earth is full of Thy possessions.

PSALM 104:24

Contents

A Little Time . . .   3

Chapter 1: World's Greatest Flower Show   5
Where I'd Take You If I Could   14

Chapter 2: Those Green Mountains   21
Where I'd Take You If I Could   36

Chapter 3: A Walk in the Woods   48
Where I'd Take You If I Could   82

Chapter 4: Patchwork Quilt   91
Back to Nature   91
The Birds and Bees   107
Where I'd Take You If I Could   123

Chapter 5: Watery World   134
Brooks and Bogs and Beaver Ponds   134
Where I'd Take You If I Could   152
Lakes and Ponds   153
Where I'd Take You If I Could   186

. . . Or Find Out for Yourself   203

Index   207

Ron Rood's
VERMONT
A Nature Guide

A Little Time . . .

There you are, with a little time to spend in our Green Mountain State. Perhaps it's a day, maybe a week. Possibly it's only an armchair trip. On the other hand, you may live here. You've had enough of superhighways and shopping carts—at least for now. It'd be nice to visit some good backcountry Vermont.

Fountains and fireworks? Leave them to places like Manhattan and Chicago and Los Angeles. There's much to learn from a little stream flinging itself over a cliff or finding its way among mossy rocks. The call of a thrush or the mumble of a porcupine talking to itself as it saunters through the woods may not be in wraparound stereo, true. But you feel a kind of excitement if you happen to be there.

You're an explorer of sorts as you come upon a trout lily by a wooded stream—or if you actually discover the trout. A deer and a deer mouse can sound the same in new-fallen autumn leaves. And the twig that just snapped: was it the wind? or was it—Something Else?

Hence this little book. Not to unsnap the twig, so to speak, but to help put you where you can hear it.

3

I'll make a few suggestions as to where you might find the track of a moose, for instance—or, if you're lucky, the great animal itself. There's the thrill of a "V" of geese overhead, the joy of finding a solitary orchid, the sobering spectacle of fullsized trees trembling in widening circles as you gingerly pick your way across a quaking bog. Such adventures can be yours, I believe, with these pages as a guide.

Peg and I have hiked and sailed and canoed our Vermont outdoors for half a lifetime. We have successfully negotiated Fat Man's Bend among the rocks at Smuggler's Notch. We're almost on speaking terms with mushroom and maple tree, bluejay and beaver. We've watched an ermine-clad weasel relentlessly pursuing a rabbit over the glittering moonlit snow. And we know what sound is made by Champ, the legendary monster of Lake Champlain. Really.

By means of this book we'll take you there. That is, if—also by means of this book—you take *us* along.

1

World's Greatest Flower Show

Where shall we start?

Well, how about where we are—or where we'd likely be at the outset of a trip—right on a Vermont road? There, at any time during the growing season, you are apt to find yourself a visitor at a tiny part of the world's biggest flower show.

Yes—the world's. You see, the show is provided by the plants that grow along our nation's miles of highways, and a great many of them are not Vermonters at all. They are not even Americans. They come from England, and France, and Africa, and the Orient.

Consider, for instance, that familiar little goldentop, the dandelion. At one time it was a stranger in these parts. So were the daisy and buttercup and the hairy-stemmed hawkweed, or devil's paintbrush. Dandelion was common in France and Belgium and other parts of Europe, where it was called *dent-de-lion*, or lion's tooth, after the jagged appearance of its leaves.

The exact date of arrival of these and other plants is not always clear, as nobody kept records. You can read about how they got here in many a pioneer diary.

DANDELION

It seems that when the settlers first arrived they found almost unbroken forest on all sides. There were no fields, no pastures, no flowery meadows. So the settlers sacrificed great trees—burned them down or merely cut and dragged them aside—to make way for those first little farms.

But you don't get a pasture overnight, and the domestic animals needed food. To fill this need the ships brought hay and forage to the New World from Europe.

The hay, of course, contained seeds. Grass seeds, yes—and seeds of dozens of weeds. Uneaten hay was used for bedding and eventually found its way to the barnyard. From there it was spread on the land with the manure. Thus duly launched, a little bit of Europe took root here in America.

There were other ways as well. Herbs and spices and entire plants were brought over to start new gardens here, or to beautify a dooryard, or merely as reminders of home. They found their way into the wild, where they became *escapes*, to use the botanical term for going native.

Then, too, ships often used loads of soil as ballast—soil that was dumped into the hold of a vessel at one end of the voyage and scooped out at the other end. This soil contained roots and seeds and bits of plants: more green colonists for America.

Today, centuries later, those leafy immigrants have joined their human neighbors as part of the landscape. They seem so natural that we figure they've always been here. And there they stand, welcoming us in the fields and along every roadside—at least, until state highway crews cut them down.

Take that go-anywhere dandelion as a starter, or the familiar white daisy. Either of these two plants alone may form a solid bank of blossoms along a highway, and you can recognize them without slacking your speed at a mile a minute.

Buttercup, another European immigrant, adds its deep-cut leaves and yellow flowers to the display. When we were children we used to hold a buttercup under each other's chin. If there was a yellow reflection from the glossy petals, it was a sure sign you liked butter. Of course it worked; butter is pretty popular with kids.

The pineapple weed is another yellow flower. Its blossoms look like the center of a little daisy without the white petals. Small as it is, the scented plant—resembling pineapple in aroma when the finely divided leaves are crushed—often makes a green mat, almost like some kind of four inch moss. It may grow along the edge of a driveway, right in the path of the lawn mower, or in the grass in the center of the drive. Thus it seems to thrive on adversity—so, even if it's not a true Vermonter, at least it's trying.

Also daisylike, with yellow center and white petals, is the mayweed. This plant forms a low roadside border most of the summer, but sniff it warily. It's an attractive little bloom, but looks can deceive. One flower book charitably allows that "its odor is unusual" and lets you take your chances. My Vermont neighbors are considerably more direct—they call it "stinkin' daisy."

Another familiar member of the daisy family is known as chicory. Its finely-ground roots are used as an additive to coffee. Chicory begins each day with blossoms of clearest blue along a tall stalk. As the day progresses the blue may fade. It's a sun-loving plant, closing when it rains—or even on a cloudy day.

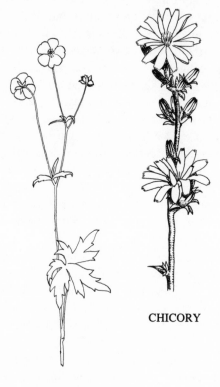

CHICORY

BUTTERCUP

Fireweed, with its tall spire of magenta-pink blossoms, has made its way over much of the world. It may be as familiar in New Zealand as in New England. It carpets meadows and mountainsides in Alaska. Fireweed often fills in where land has been cleared or burned—hence its name. Whole fields and roadsides sometimes seem a solid mass of pink with its chest-high spears.

Often taller than fireweed is the mullein, or flannel plant. Its large velvety leaves look and feel like cloth. From its basal rosette a slender spire arises, bearing clusters of buds and a few yellow flowers. Even in winter you may notice these spires. As much as six feet tall, they are dead but still staunchly erect in the snow.

You may like to make the acquaintance of butter-and-eggs, colored as its name indicates. Gently squeeze the blossoms of this attractive little wild snapdragon and its petals open in a hearty yawn. It's a mid- to late-summer plant, as are the roadside thistles, with shaving brush flowers of pink or blue—plus their prickly foliage.

Creeping vetch sometimes invades the roadbanks from a nearby field. It has tendril-tipped stems and rows of little purple-blue blossoms in pairs. Vetch often makes blotches of color in a green meadow. Its wiry stems also bring forth colorful language from the farmer: the plant can make a fine tangle for the mowing machine.

There's also the tawny orange of the tall day lilies with tomorrow's buds ready to replace today's shortlived blooms. Bees and other insects sometimes bite through those buds to get an early sample of the flower's nectar.

The common dock is less colorful. Once it was less common, too, but helpful bulldozers and road machinery have spread it everywhere. Look for a plant with a spike of crowded tiny green flowers, large leaves, and a deep taproot. Find it along sandy roadsides or in the middle of your choicest flower bed: the common dock isn't at all fussy.

Look for another stowaway from early times: the burdock, whose clustered little heads of delicate lavender belie the bristly, hooked burrs that hitch a ride on your sweater or your dog's coat. Those clinging burrs find their modern counterpart in today's Velcro, used to help close almost anything that's open.

BURDOCK

Add to these the shredded-looking ragweed, whose little green blossoms supply enough windborne pollen to satisfy the most dedicated hay fever buff, and it becomes quite an array indeed. All of these are Vermonters by accident, so to speak, rather than by ancestry.

Even our state flower, the red clover, came here as a tourist. It was brought over by early colonists as a forage crop. The same is true of the little white clover, so common in our lawns.

RED CLOVER

Both may add their talents to that multi-mile display. They may be joined by another escape from the feedlot: the tall alfalfa, with blue or violet flowers and longish cloverlike leaves.

Indeed, history is still in the making. One modern escape of this century is birdsfoot trefoil. Popular in recent years as a forage crop, its intensely yellow cloverlike blooms add color to our roadsides. Its little seeds are borne in several skinny pods arranged like the toes of a bird's foot: hence its name. The seeds, dropped from a farmer's wagon, leave a record of the vehicle's passing for years to come.

The grasses fed to those pioneer animals have also left a legacy. Their descendants populate hayfield and highway edge alike. Timothy, ryegrass, orchard grass, and that gardener's delight, crabgrass, got their start in the old world. Kentucky bluegrass, too, can be traced back to European farms and fields.

A number of our garden flowers and vegetables also claim a dual allegiance. Corn and tobacco came here from Central and South America. So did potatoes, tomatoes, peppers and many of our melons and squashes. Some mustards are native to Asia while at least one variety of hops originated in Japan.

The names of Swiss chard, Brussels sprouts, and Chinese cabbage suggest their ancestry. Peas and beans and turnips also came from Europe. Parsley apparently originated along the Mediterranean coast. Oats, barley, and some kinds of wheat probably got their start in North Africa.

Even that familiar shrub of our dooryard, the lilac, goes back to Europe—and thence, possibly to Asia. As with other landscape and garden plants, it may be left to its own devices. Many a forgotten home foundation, half filled in with soil and leaves, is still marked by a sentinel in the form of a faithful lilac bush.

Indeed, one holdover from less hurried days greeted me unexpectedly on a visit to the Air Guard Station in Burlington. On a grassy slope near the jet maintenance building bloomed a little golden bouquet. It was a birdsfoot trefoil plant, trimmed to four inches by the mower, peacefully spreading a score of sunny blossoms—right beneath the nose of a F-102 delta wing fighter mounted on a pedestal high above it.

Drive or hike or bike along almost any highway and enjoy a generous portion of this flower show for yourself. I'd suggest a little road, where you can go along at your own pace. Then you won't have to listen to somebody blowing a horn, or see someone glaring accusingly in your rear view mirror.

That's one virtue of our superhighways, I believe: they take the pressure off the lesser roads. These latter now are more enjoyable and comfortable than they've been for years.

In suggesting *which* smaller roads to take, I'd recommend those where the town has yet to clear the roadside greenery for the summer. Or you could hope things might turn out as they did in one little Vermont village.

It seems the selectmen contracted with a local handyman to go over the roadsides with his mower. Away he went, the toothed cutter bar on his tractor chattering its eagerness to get at the weeds. Trouble was, the bar didn't have some of its teeth, so about all he did was comb the plants.

"Wal," he drawled when faced with the ragged results of his task, "you asked me to go over the roadsides with my tractor. So I done it."

Where I'd Take You If I Could

Pownal-Bennington-Arlington Loop. There's scarcely a Vermont road that doesn't share in the state's big floral display from April to November. One of my favorite drives takes a look at centuries of past use by horse-drawn vehicles and foot travelers alike. It's that well-worn stretch of highway leading north from Pownal, on the Massachusetts border, along the southwestern edge of Vermont.

The road has long served as an avenue for farmers and explorers and adventurers as they spread northward. Formerly U.S. Route 7, it has been relegated to the status of 7A north of Bennington with the opening of an impressive new highway a few miles to the east, the present U.S. 7. The older road—renamed, perhaps a bit apologetically, now that it's been supplanted by the new highway—is labeled "Historic 7A."

As you travel this venerable thoroughfare, you can imagine a farm wagon scattering weed seeds as it takes a fragrant load of hay to the barn. You can see the patient horses and oxen as they relieve themselves along the way: more potential greenery in the form of undigested seeds. A discarded apple core, a chewed-on stalk of grass tossed aside by a farm youngster— still more vegetation.

Many such events are recorded today along that road. Optimistic dandelions bloom there as early as March. They're followed by buttercup, daisy, alfalfa, clover and chicory—to name a few. Later in the summer you find the tall, spreading plant known as knapweed, with small slender leaves and attractive pinkish ragged-looking flowers.

The round trip takes about an hour and a half of driving. Follow U.S. Route 7, then U.S. 7A north from Pownal to Bennington to Arlington. This latter town was the home of artist Norman Rockwell and writer Dorothy Canfield Fisher.

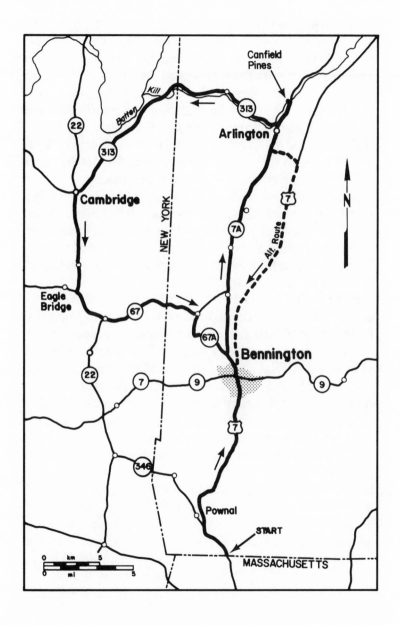

Your road is about to turn west on Vermont 313, but a two-mile foray northward is well worth the effort. This will allow a visit to the Canfield grove—among the largest white pines in all our northeast. Take the second left off Route 7A about two miles north of Arlington: the pines are in a forty-acre grove near the end of the half-mile road. Some are nearly three feet in diameter and well over a hundred feet tall.

If you visited the Canfield pines, retrace your steps to Route 313 west (right) out of Arlington. This road follows the Batten Kill, one of the northeast's famous trout streams.

About a mile from Arlington, look for a plaque on the right marking the site of the state seal pine on a hill alongside Route 313. Nearly six feet in diameter, this was one of North America's largest white pines. A few years ago it crashed to earth, but its likeness still adorns the official Vermont state seal, much as it was designed by Ira Allen back in 1778.

If you're a purist about remaining in Vermont, make a U-turn at the New York border and retrace your steps to Route 7A. Follow it south about a mile from Arlington and turn east (left) onto the access to the modern Route 7. Take this new road back to Bennington—and note the absence of many roadside flowers. This highway has but recently been carved out of the woodland, so it lacks the variety that history would give it. But better look quick: hay and straw used to prevent slope erosion may soon colonize those roadside shoulders.

If you cross the Vermont-New York border on Route 313, you'll see more of this far-flung flower show. In July, for instance, the wet meadows and roadside ditches are filled with the slender spires of purple loosestrife—prized in English gardens as Long Purples. It's regarded as a weed here, but would add a striking magenta touch to some little wet area of your own.

Continuing southwest on Route 313, you join New York 22 at Cambridge. Along these roads, as on many northeastern byways in summer, the field edges may be canopied with thousands of little umbrellas: the flat-topped clusters of wild carrot or Queen Anne's lace.

More exquisite than any hand-sewn doily, each of these white discs may measure up to five inches across. It is borne above the meadow on a spindly, branched stem two or three feet high. In the center of the disc you'll occasionally find a dark red blob about the size of one of the hundreds of tiny blossoms—the drop of blood that fell when the royal lacemaker pricked her finger with the needle.

About six miles south of Cambridge on Route 22, turn east on Route 67 near Eagle Bridge. Follow it to 67A and thence back to Bennington. You'll have driven a circle through the variety of a scattered fifty-mile flower garden.

QUEEN ANNE'S LACE

Orange-Windsor Loop. If we had the chance, you and I, we could spot dozens of kinds of flowering immigrants along almost any route. Vermont highways, many of them, began as farm roads or even cattle paths, and the plants along the way show it. You may see many such plants along the circle that could also be called the Orange-Windsor loop, after the two counties it traverses.

The loop is somewhat less than two hours' driving time but I'm not allowing for stops. It begins on U.S. Route 5, headed north out of White River Junction. This route accompanies the Connecticut River upstream. Along the way it passes little towns and shops with local produce and native crafts.

If you look, you'll also find the aftermath of travel by visitors who preceded you by two centuries and more. Here and there are a few plants that, like many another Vermont resident, have deserted life on the farm. We've discovered asparagus on a sandy roadside near Pompanoosuc, for instance, and a few volunteer stalks of buckwheat. There's even an occasional tobacco plant. Its relatives are more at home in the rich broad valley of the river about two hundred miles downstream in Connecticut and Massachusetts.

Turn northwest off Route 5 at Bradford onto Route 25. Follow 25 about five miles to the town highway that turns left (west) toward the tiny hamlets of South Corinth (pronounced by many residents with the accent on the last syllable) and Goose Green (pronounced Goose Green). Continue to Route 113; turn right and travel the next four miles along a little stream with the interesting name of Jail Brook.

Jail Brook joins a branch of the White River (First Branch, it's called) at the lovely village of Chelsea. Route 113 joins Route 110 there, too. Taking Route 110 to the left you follow this branch of the White River south, passing on the way through Tunbridge, site of the rip-roaring annual September Tunbridge World's Fair. If you're interested in covered bridges you'll find

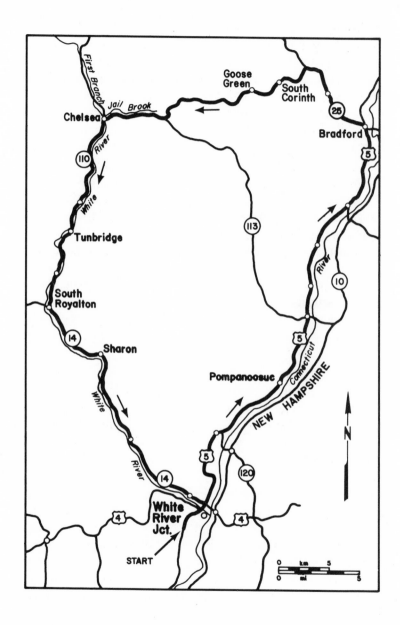

19

half a dozen of them on your way to Route 14 at South Royalton.

At this point the White River gains its maturity after having been joined by several watercourses upstream. It tumbles southeast toward the Connecticut River and the Junction that bears its name. Route 14, accompanying it, takes you through steep-sided valleys and past more flower-lined roadsides and back to White River Junction once more.

These are but two suggested routes. Or, if you have a touch of the maverick in you, do as Peg and I often do: pack a lunch and pick out a road on the map. Then discover your own primrose path (some primroses are visitors who never went back home, either).

So there you could be, greeting old friends like roadside daisies and dandelions with perhaps a new appreciation. And all this time you thought they were as American as apple pie.

Well, actually, you were right. Apples, it seems, aren't native here either. Scientists say they got their start in southwestern Asia.

2

Those Green Mountains

It's but a step, so to speak, from Vermont's green-bordered highways to its green-mantled mountains. Worn down over eons of time, our mountains are but rounded nubbins of peaks that once soared higher than the Rockies. They're so much a part of our state that the very name *Vermont* is related to two French words, *vert* and *mont*: green and mountain.

Those mountains form the state's backbone northward from Massachusetts to Canada, with other knobs and bulges right and left. (There's the Taconic Range in the southwest corner, for instance.) Such terrain doubtless gave rise to the mythical Vermont cows with shorter legs on one side so they could graze the hilly pastures. Today their less gifted descendants still create bovine terraced pathways; you can see them winding around hillsides, following the same level like contour lines on a map.

In spite of Vermont's corrugated configuration, however, there is no truth to the old timer's feeling that "if you pulled all the damn wrinkles out, it'd be bigger'n Texas." The Lone Star State, it seems, has some fairly sizeable mountains of its own.

VERMONT COW

Almost any east-west road takes you eventually to the mountains. It nearly has to, with some eighty percent of the state classified as hilly. The juncture of hill and highway is sometimes honored by a picturesque title: Hazen's Notch, for instance, or Brandon Gap or Sherburne Pass. There's usually parking at such places so you can abandon the car and walk the ridges yourself.

At Sherburne Pass, for instance, the Long Trail and the Appalachian Trail divide. The pass is about ten miles east of Rutland on U.S. Route 4. After sharing a common route northward from Williamstown at the Massachusetts border, the two hiking systems meet the highway and diverge—the Long Trail heads north to Canada; the Appalachian goes east to Maine.

The Green Mountain Club maintains and preserves the Long Trail, "A Footpath in the Wilderness" as it is called. The trail is well kept, although volunteer help and funds are always needed. It is there to welcome you at many a mountain pass, inviting you to walk an hour or a week. A map and guidebook are available from the Club at P.O. Box 889, Montpelier, Vermont 05602.

The "green" part of the Green Mountains is a result of an average of thirty to forty inches of precipitation per year—in the lower areas, that is. The trees on the higher peaks gain a good share of their moisture by combing the clouds.

MISTED EVERGREENS

s the incessant winds, driving the fog and mist of the upper air before them, run smack into the needles of the mountaintop evergreens. Water droplets in the moisture-laden clouds are actually shaken loose by the impact and cling to the needles. The rest of the cloud passes on. Often your hair or sweater may get drenched in the same way up there. You can see these self-watering trees on many a mountaintop, glittering with ten thousand liquid jewels. Yet not a drop of rain is falling.

Wind and water reduced these Vermont peaks to their present level. The water came not only as droplets in clouds and storms but in crystals of ice—and in the great ice sheets that have periodically invaded from the north. A mile thick in places, the latest glacier reached its greatest advance some eighteen thousand years ago. Grinding and scraping, it carried rocks and soil and tree trunks as it plowed ahead.

Gripped by the ice, a moving boulder might gouge a furrow in the solid bedrock. Such glacial grooves, running north and south, can sometimes be seen on a bare mountain ledge. Occasionally a rock will still be at the end of the scrape it created, even though the glacier that dragged the rock there retreated more than ten thousand years ago.

GLACIAL GROOVE IN LEDGE

Actually, "retreated" is not quite the word. As the climate warmed, the pile-up of ice further north diminished. The glacier's forward motion ceased. There it lay, slowly melting and abandoning its load on the spot.

Eventually the ice disappeared. The land became clothed in green once more. Today we may think little of the roundness of ice-scraped hills. We scarcely realize the origin of today's gravel pits—many of them ancient sandbars left by glacial streams. We take for granted the wideness of valleys reamed out by the glacier (you drive through one such valley from Bennington to Rutland on old U.S. Route 7) and the number of rocks with which Vermont is abundantly blessed—some of these rocks having been dragged and pushed here from as far away as Canada.

Now and again one of these boulders, abandoned by the glacier, causes you to contemplate its unlikely presence in the middle of a forest, say, or out in a meadow. Such a glacial erratic, as it is called, may be larger than a truck. One line of these erratics extends south from Mt. Ascutney, near Windsor. Known as the Ascutney Train, it's an assortment of boulders snatched off the top of the mountain and scattered clear down into Massachusetts.

Near the summit of 4,052-foot Mt. Abraham in Lincoln, a spheroid of milky quartz gleams a welcome to hikers on the Long Trail. There's only conjecture as to where it came from, and doubtless many people have considered removing it to a rock garden, say, or the middle of some lucky lawn. But the great white boulder is undisturbed—it's as big as a bear and weighs several tons.

The exposed surface of many cliffs and peaks is often of a material known as schist. You can find it for yourself on a mountain pass or where a highway cuts through the rocks. It is often gray-green, layered in structure, and frequently contains glistening flakes of mica. Schist is crumbly and tends to split off

GLACIAL ERRATIC

in layers or chunks, giving rise to those "Watch for Falling Rock" signs along the road.

Besides the dense white quartz and soft gray schist you may see a coarse, granular rock known as gneiss (pronounced "nice"). It's composed of several scattered or layered minerals, giving a pepper-and-salt appearance. Gneiss resembles the familiar but much harder granite; you can see countless tons of the latter in the area of the world's largest granite quarries near Barre. The name Barre, by the way, rhymes with carry—and Vermont granite has, indeed, been carried worldwide.

In many parts of the Champlain Valley you'll find limestone, its white color telling of the marine shells that gave it its origin. You can also see marble, which is limestone changed by heat and pressure. Limestone occurs along much of U.S. Route 7, while marble is quarried in areas such as Proctor, west of Rutland.

In the region of Danby and Wallingford you'll see chunks of limestone piled up into walls. These, just as with the many stone walls that form a network over rural Vermont, serve two purposes: they help keep livestock in place, and, as my neighbor says, "they get the danged rocks out of the fields."

To add to the rockpile, so to speak, you can find acres of gray-black shale along the shores of Lake Champlain. Shale is formed of layers of compressed clay and easily splits into thin sheets. Wave-worn chips of shale make wonderful bouncing pebbles to skitter out across the water.

A stronger material, slate, is found in the Taconic Mountain and Bomoseen areas of southwestern Vermont—in Poultney and Fair Haven, for instance. There's talc and asbestos in the vicinity of Johnson and Lowell. Copper ore can be found near Vershire, Strafford, and Thetford. Brick-colored jasper, once used for arrowheads, occurs around Colchester.

Add to these and many other native materials all the gravel and boulders hauled in by the glacier, and you can find samples of almost any northeastern rock in Vermont if you look long enough. I mentioned this to one of my Vermont neighbors and he agreed. "You sure can," he said, "and most of them right in my pasture."

The rocks, and the soil created from them, have a bearing on the kinds of living things in a region. So does the climate, of course, especially in the mountainous state of Vermont. The plants that can survive in the thin mountain air need to be able to huddle close to the ground, away from the wind. Their daily needs must be met by the thin soils, rocky terrain and wild changes in weather of those upper altitudes.

Suppose we begin at the bottom of Vermont's stony backbone and work our way up to those windswept slopes. Our mountains are host to a wealth of life, and just to name them all would make this book as thick as a New York City telephone directory. We'll just take a few that could become old friends—and regret we cannot cover them all.

We could start our imaginary walk with that aromatic evergreen, the balsam fir. It occurs all the way from the lower woods to timberline. Its flattened, round-pointed needles are soft and wonderfully fragrant. Indeed, they're often used to make the "pine pillows" sold in gift shops.

Pull a needle from a balsam twig and it leaves a flat, round scar. Other evergreens leave tiny stumps or ragged splinters. Balsam cones stand erect on the branch, while most other evergreen cones hang downwards. Canada balsam, the sticky resin found in soft blisters on the trunk, makes a fine glue when it dries. Clear and colorless, it was long used as a cement to hold components together in optical instruments, as it allowed light to pass through without distortion.

Spruce resembles balsam, but the needles are stiffer and more prickly. Our common species, the red spruce, often gives up the mountain climb before the balsam, but at lower altitudes the two species have the same Christmas tree appearance when young.

Older spruce has brown-black scaly bark, whereas that of balsam is smoother and lighter gray. Spruce resin, dried after oozing from a wound in the bark, can be used as a pungent chewing gum—or so my neighbors say. Personally, I cannot stand the stuff.

The lower mountain slopes are also home to the tree known as eastern hemlock. As with the balsam, the flat needles have tips that are rounded or even slightly notched. The foliage has a two-ranked, flattened appearance. The tip of a hemlock curves over in a graceful arc; it's not stiffly upright as with most other evergreen trees.

Peg and I often bring a hemlock into our home for a Christmas tree. Its drooping branches lend to a graceful touch, and its many little needles make it look almost as if it was already decorated.

EASTERN HEMLOCK

These needles drop readily if the tree dries out, by the way, so we make sure the cut end of the trunk is fresh. Then we skin off the botton two inches of bark for good absorption and stand the trunk in a container of water. It'll drink a quart or more daily, putting the water back into the room for much-needed humidity. Such treatment, incidentally, is good for almost any Christmas tree.

The hemlock's flexible tip helps you tell it from most other evergreens except the cedars. There are two common but unrelated species of cedar, red and white. They are trees more of hillsides than mountains, but they're often mixed with the others so we'll cover them here.

White cedar's scalelike leaves, folded against the twig, give the drooping foliage a flattened appearance. Also known as arborvitae, white cedar provides good winter food for animals. It provides good cover, as well, and arborvitae swamps may become deer yards during the snow season. Your ornamental arborvitae with its tasty twigs may become a rabbit yard, too, even if you didn't plan it that way.

Darker than the yellow-green of arborvitae, the slender or branching red cedar is more common to open fields and pastures. Its fruit looks like small blueberries in contrast to the tiny clustered cones of white cedar. Red cedar leaves may be scale-like or short and pointed. The tree's little cousin, the juniper, has similar leaves and fruit, but it's a low, spreading bush. Red cedar or juniper berries, incidentally, are used in the making of gin—for whatever value that information may be to you.

Your cedar chest is probably made of red cedar. Either species may be used for posts, shingles, and siding. A sniff of a new-sharpened pencil tells you one more use for red cedar.

Cedars, spruces, firs, and hemlocks have needles borne singly on the twig rather than in bunches like pine and tamarack. Our eastern white pine has soft three-inch needles in bundles of five, so the tree is easy to identify. The knotty pine paneling in your home is probably of white pine, as are a number of shelves and cabinets—indeed, many kinds of construction.

The needles of red pine, two in a bunch, may be four to six inches long. Also called Norway pine, this species is native in spite of its name. It grows fast and well, even on poor soils. Hence it is often used in reforestation. As you drive the Vermont countryside you'll see large plots of red pine planted in rows and growing as much as two feet in height per year.

A handy way to arrive at the age of an evergreen is to count the whorls, or groups of branches, arranged at intervals up the main trunk. Each whorl of six or eight branches indicates a year's growth. Thus a tree with twenty whorls is at least twenty years old. The figure is only approximate, however, as lower branches may drop off with hardly a trace.

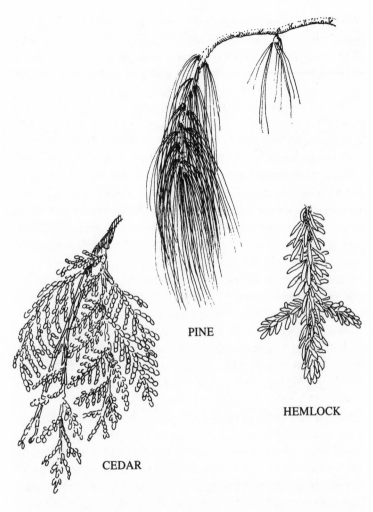

PINE

HEMLOCK

CEDAR

The tamarack, or larch, looks like other evergreens but with tufts of six or more half-inch needles along the branch. These needles turn yellow and drop in the fall—doubtless a bit disconcerting to someone who goes back to cut the Christmas tree picked out earlier in the year.

Part way up the mountain trail you are joined by the heart-leaved birch. This tree, the highland variety of the white or paper birch, stays with you on the upward climb until it retires in favor of fir and spruce. The bark has its down-country cousin's ability to peel off in thin strips or thick layers, but the leaves are different in appearance. Instead of having the outline of an egg (ovate), they are known as cordate, which is—you guessed it—heart shaped.

There are various broadleaved trees such as other birches and maples on mountainsides; we'll meet them in the woodlands chapter. One old friend you may find is worth mentioning here, the American mountain ash. You've probably known this small tree as an ornamental. Perhaps you have one on your own lawn, with compound leaves (several leaflets on a single stem) and clusters of orange-red berrylike fruit.

After watching a flock of grosbeaks feeding greedily on mountain ash, I decided to try some for myself. The fruit is—well, interesting—sort of like apple cores dipped in lemon juice.

One plant you'll be happy to discover on the upper trails is the mountain blueberry. It's a low creeping bush with elliptical leaves. Its pink or white blossoms look like waxy little bells, and toward summer's end it rewards the hiker with those tasty berries.

Blueberries will often stay with you to the bald mountain top. Indeed, mountain tops are fine, as they provide plenty of sunlight, lack of competition and, often, the acid soil needed by this species. A friend of mine has suggested, tongue in cheek, that we in the northeast should go into the blueberry business. The plants would be bountifully and healthfully watered, he says, by acid rain.

Mountaintop trees are sometimes draped with an oddball plant known as Old Man's Beard. Wispy gray and straggly, it hangs like the Spanish moss of southern states. Old Man's Beard is

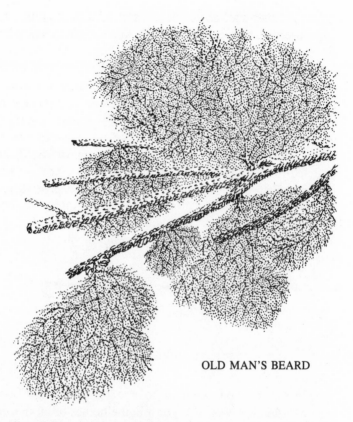

OLD MAN'S BEARD

actually a lichen, related to the gray crusts on rocks, while Spanish moss is a distant cousin of the pineapple. Neither species harms the tree; it merely uses it for support.

On the highest peaks such as Mansfield and Camel's Hump you can find a few acres of genuine Arctic tundra. This tundra is a relict of that glacial age ten thousand and more years ago. It's a fragile region, and the alpine plants living there have but a shaky hold on life. Tread gingerly in these tundra areas. Even a footstep among those sedges, bilberries, mountain cranberries, and other species can be a disaster, so stay on the trail. Otherwise you may destroy the very life that makes a high peak so special.

Most mountain wildlife can be found in lower regions as well; you'll meet them in later chapters. One you may encounter on those high slopes is the little shrew. This tiny mammal, intent on its eternal quest for food, may busily scamper right over to the toe of your shoe. It may even take an experimental nibble—just in case the shoe is edible, I suppose. Sometimes as it scurries about, the shrew talks to itself in a string of high-pitched squeaks, sounding like the hiss of escaping steam.

SHREW

A shrew may be neighbor to one of several species of mouse—and an unwelcome guest in the homes of all of them. Shrews may look like mice, but that's where the similarity stops. Mice are larger than the shrew; the latter may be no bigger than your thumb. Mice also have conspicuous eyes and ears as well as those typical chisel-like front teeth. The teeth of a shrew are sharp and pointed, almost like little needles. The animal is good at using them, too—on mice or insects or almost anything else.

Especially tuned to the winds and wildness of the upper slopes is that largest American member of the crow family, the northern raven. A third larger than its familiar cousin of the cornfield, the raven shares the crow's coloration and general appearance. The larger bird's central tailfeathers extend farther than its side feathers, thus giving its nether appendage a somewhat elongated shape.

It's in manner of flight that the raven often differs markedly from the crow. Crows travel from point A to point B in a relatively straight line and with apparent determination—as the crow flies, one might say. Ravens make an adventure of it. A raven will be flapping along, uttering its distinctive guttural "kronk!" when it suddenly does a flip. Over on one side it goes, then wildly to the other. Sometimes it tumbles earthward as if shot.

Two ravens playing on the wing look like an aerial dogfight. At other times they'll soar on the mountain updrafts like a toy kite, scarcely moving a feather. Once on Mt. Mansfield a raven hung motionless out over the slope in front of me for several minutes. The only perceptible movement was its head as it casually looked about from its unparalleled perch on the winds rising from the valley below.

During migration, birds of many species follow the ridges. They may feed during the day and fly at night. Sometimes we can hear them chirping on the distant slopes long after dark. When I mentioned this nonstop activity to a third grade class and wondered aloud how they could do it, one youngster had the answer. "I guess," he said, "they must fly in their sleep."

Chances are you'll meet other creatures along the mountain trails: blue jays, for instance, the chipmunks and even a porcupine. Rather than introduce them twice, however, I'll save them for later chapters. Many of them are opportunists anyway and take their living where they find it—regardless of where the book says they are supposed to be.

Where I'd Take You If I Could

To Mount Abraham and Back. You might expect I'd be most familiar with the mountain trails near my home in Lincoln. So I am—and so are many of the 100,000 vacationists who travel a portion of the Long Trail each year.

The Lincoln ridge hike I'm about to suggest is one of the most popular of the entire 260 miles of the Trail. If there's some way you can have a vehicle pick you up, you can do all but about three quarters of a mile of this hike without once backtracking. A car lets you out at Lincoln Gap, then drives seven miles to the Battell trailhead in the eastern part of town. There you should appear about three hours, and five-plus miles, later. (Directions to the trailhead appear on page 39.)

Without such motorized accommodations you'd probably best retrace your steps—Lincoln Gap to Mt. Abraham and back. Peg and I have done just that more than a dozen times. From Mt. Abraham's summit, the sweeping view of the Adirondacks, the Green Mountains, Lake Champlain, and three states is one of the best panoramas on the entire Long Trail.

You'll need fairly sturdy shoes for the three-mile hike to the summit, although I've done it in sneakers. It's windy and cool at 4,052 feet, even on the most summery day, so consider yourself forewarned.

There's space for about two dozen cars at Lincoln Gap, which is about 4½ miles from the center of Lincoln on the road between Lincoln and Warren. The Long Trail crosses at this height (2,424 feet) on its way between Massachusetts and Canada.

We'll consider the hike to Mt. Abraham, on your left (north) as you cross the gap from the direction of Lincoln. But, if you go right (south) on the trail, you'll have fine views toward New York and the Adirondacks from cliffs within the first mile. You

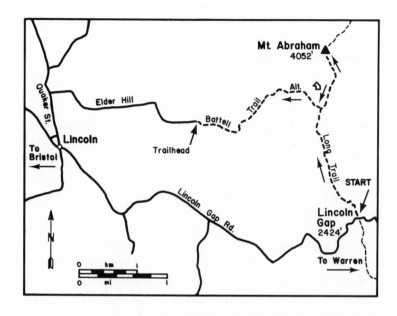

may also encounter a few peppery plants. Woodland nettles grow close to your unsuspecting legs as you trudge along. Their toothed leaves are borne on a fuzzy stem—but don't touch. That fuzz is really thousands of tiny needles just waiting to make your acquaintance. Luckily they cannot penetrate normal clothing. Luckily, too, the sting is short-lived, so by the time you reach Lookout Cliff you'll probably be cured.

There are few, if any, nettles on the northern trail. Traveling in this direction toward Mt. Abraham you'll run the gamut of almost every native Vermont woodland tree, shrub, and herb. There are yellow violets at the gap, plus red trillium and the brown-streaked hoods of the green jack-in-the-pulpit in spring. Later in the season the roadside is covered with pale touch-me-not. The yellow flowers of this plant mature into little seed capsules that snap apart at the slightest contact—hence the name.

Here you're on the rocky spine of the Green Mountains. Along the road on the steep western side you can see white quartz boulders scattered on the banks. There are also a few of these boulders as you begin the trail.

The first portion of the pathway is fairly level, with occasional ups and downs. Your small green companions will include a number of plants described more fully in the next chapter: witch hobble, Christmas fern, ground dogwood or bunchberry, and Clintonia with its startlingly blue fruit on a green stalk. The medium-sized mountain ash is here, too, with its compound leaves and orange-red berries. So are most of the forest trees dealt with in the next chapter: maples, beech, shadbush, black cherry, and striped maple.

After a few hundred yards the trail begins to climb. White birch and red spruce join the sylvan aggregation, accompanied by a few balsam fir. The prickly spruce and the softer-needled fir will be your companions almost continually for the next couple of miles to the Battell Shelter. The shelter is a lean-to maintained by the Green Mountain Club.

You have a fine chance of meeting a porcupine along the way. We've seen the big, placid rodents several times. Chipmunks are there, too, along with their chatterbox cousins, the red squirrels. You may notice a white-footed mouse as well—by sound, if not by sight, as the little creature often makes an astonishing racket in the dry leaves.

Listen for the croak of a raven as you travel. The big birds, looking like outsized crows, make their nests on windy, rocky ledges. Ruffed grouse take flight and thunder off through the trees, while little dark gray juncos flit across the trail—each one showing the white sides of its tail as it flies. White-throated sparrows sound their clear whistle, and black-capped chickadees accompany you on your walk—ostensibly inspecting the greenery but, I believe, also inspecting *you*.

The first two miles might be classed as easy to moderate in

terms of difficulty. Log steps have been placed here and there, while at least one strategic handrail helps you over a tricky spot. As you go upward, the broad-leaved trees gradually diminish until you're largely in an evergreen forest. Here the scraggly lichen "Old Man's Beard" is draped over many of the trees.

About two miles from your start at Lincoln Gap the Battell Trail joins you from the left. This is the pathway you may take if there's a car waiting for you at the bottom. (To reach Battell Trailhead, seven miles from Lincoln Gap by car, turn up Quaker Street in the center of town past the church and town clerk's office. About six tenths of a mile from the center, turn right onto Elder Hill. Follow this gravel road two miles to the small wooded parking area identified by signs indicating the start of the trail.)

Meanwhile, back on the main trail, you soon reach Battell Shelter, three quarters of a mile from the top. There's a flowing spring a few yards away, while primitive toilet facilities are in another nearby area. There's usually a log book for you to sign, but be sure to return it to its proper place. Otherwise a "porky" may chew it to bits.

Once past the shelter, the trail gets steeper. Spruce and fir, stunted by the winds at this altitude, poke up from the ledges and around large rocks. Half the time you're walking; the other half you're clambering upward. It's a difficult pathway but not dangerous. Indeed, you can stop almost anywhere and enjoy a view that widens with every few steps.

Most of the vegetation gives up the struggle near the top. Blueberries no longer make ankle-deep mats on the thin soil. Century-old firs, gnarled, twisted, and thick with blue-green foliage, look like head-high bonsai trees. The wind sighs and whistles through their needles and between the rocks as it races across this bald summit and out over the valley. Little grass-like sedges, lichens, and mosses cling to their precarious footing.

Be careful as you move about to enjoy the spectacular view

here on Potato Hill, as Mt. Abraham is also called. Some of these plants are more at home hundreds of miles further north. Once crushed or uprooted, they may take scores of years to recover—if they come back at all.

The return trip takes you over and around those rugged rocks again—including the large white boulder I mentioned earlier in this chapter. The trees seem to take heart as they drop down from the zone of wind and cloud, and soon they resume a more normal shape and size. Then, in perhaps a third of the time it took to climb, you're back at Lincoln Gap.

If you're descending the two miles of the Battell Trail you'll be following a stream bed in many places. The zones of vegetation change as you descend: fir to spruce to broad-leaved trees. Christmas ferns add their dark green to the lighter color of our native shamrock, sour clover or wood sorrel. At the bottom of the trail are alders with their speckled, dark green bark, poplars (lighter green bark), gray birch, and—you hope—that waiting car.

There's an extinct farm near the end of the Battell Trail. You'll find little more than a brushy field or two to mark it, plus an overgrown beaver meadow. Look for woodchucks along the fence lines; I've also seen a red fox trotting along the road. There's another reward waiting along the roadside, if there's been enough rainfall and it's toward the end of summer. In spite of the thorns it's worth the effort: a handful of glistening, sun-warmed wild blackberries.

If time and energy do not permit a hike on the ridges, there's another way to climb a mountain, of course. This involves America's favorite mechanical toy, the automobile.

Mountain Pass Loop. One tour I have in mind gives samples of views from on high plus a look at the stuff the hills are made of. We work our way from one of Vermont's lowest points and across a mountain pass. You could even visit a granite

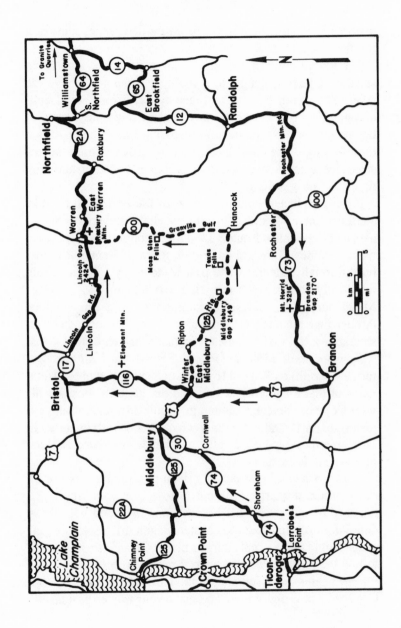

quarry if you have the time. The entire drive takes most of a morning or afternoon.

The lowest point of this one hundred fifty-mile loop is the surface of Lake Champlain, some ninety-plus feet above sea level. You can make your entrance by ferry from Fort Ticonderoga, New York, or you may begin a few miles north, at Chimney Point, Vermont, after crossing Lake Champlain on the toll bridge. The ferry, by the way, is guided across a narrow stretch of water by means of twin cables that wind up and drop down as you go along.

From Larrabee's Point (terminus of the Fort Ti ferry) take Vermont Route 74 north and east through the orchards of Shoreham and Cornwall to Route 30 and Middlebury. If you approach from Chimney Point and its bridge, Route 125 enters Middlebury through valleyland and past Middlebury College. From this lovely college town turn right (south) on U.S. 7 to East Middlebury, four miles. In summertime you can continue through high mountain terrain, but in winter there are other considerations: "closed" signs, for instance, and eight-foot drifts.

Summer Route through Lincoln Gap. At East Middlebury, turn left (north) on Route 116 past woodlands, gravel pits (remnants of that long-ago glacier), and the jumbled rocks on the west slope of Elephant Mountain. Route 116 joins Route 17; turn right on 17 and enter the town of Bristol with its little village green, stagecoach display and bandstand (concert Wednesday nights in summer).

Follow Route 17 east out of Bristol past the famous Lord's Prayer rock, a quarter mile out of town, on your right. The flat face of this pyramidal boulder was inscribed with those familiar words years ago to chasten wagon drivers whose language would make a muleskinner blush. Go another mile, then follow the river gorge upstream through Lincoln.

Now begins the mountain climb. Turn left onto the Lincoln Gap road a mile out of town and make your way up past farms, woods and rocky ledges. At the Gap itself, 2,424 feet high, you'll find quartz boulders, plus layers of schist in the rock cut.

Park at the Gap, Vermont's highest paved public highway. Walk east or west along the highway a few hundred yards to glimpse spectacular views through the trees in either direction. Then, with your car in lowest gear, begin the descent to Warren, and its little covered bridge over the Mad River.

Go through this little bridge, and you're in Warren in less than a mile. Turn right (east) in the village center and follow the town highway toward East Warren and climb over Roxbury Mountain. As you ascend the gravel road, you'll glimpse mountain slopes and a few ski trails behind you and to the left. You'll also have a chance to contemplate a sailplane or two in the sky—riding the same updrafts that carry hawks and ravens aloft.

At Roxbury you're in the geographical center of Vermont. Turn north (left) here on Route 12A toward Northfield, then sharply south (right) in about seven miles to the town with the interesting name of South Northfield. Head east again on Route 64 to Williamstown. Here, if you wish, you may drive five miles further east to the famous granite quarries near Foxville, Websterville, and Graniteville.

From Williamstown, turn south on Route 14 to the junction with Route 65 at East Brookfield. About two miles west, in Brookfield, is the famous floating bridge. You can drive or walk across this unique buoyant raft, which is actually a part of the highway.

Three miles after crossing the bridge you encounter Route 12 in a sharp turn to the south (left). Follow Route 12 about fifteen miles to still another mountain turnoff, the Rochester Mountain road, headed west (on your right).

Again you'll go uphill and down, alternating gravel and blacktop, to the town of Rochester and Route 100. Go one mile south and veer to your right (west) onto Route 73. You'll pass the picturesque rock-cliffed hill with the startling name of Mount Horrid. Continue through Brandon Gap to Brandon and U.S. 7. A right turn north on U.S. 7 brings you back to Middlebury in about twenty minutes.

Winter route through Middlebury Gap. (Also part of the Watery World tour, later, so don't worry if you miss it now.) The old timer's comment, "If I was going there I wouldn't start from here," holds especially true for many mountain passes in winter. You are apt to be up to your ears in snow—that is, if you can find the road at all; thus the reason the Lincoln Gap is closed in the winter. The alternate route continues from East Middlebury on Route 125 to Ripton, a home of Robert Frost. Climb past the Snow Bowl ski area to Middlebury Gap (open in winter), then drop down the winding road to Hancock.

Before you reach Hancock, you'll pass the entrance to Texas Falls on your left (north), toward the bottom of the descent. It's a fine little river gorge and one of our favorite summer picnic areas. About four miles further the road joins Route 100 at Hancock. Turn left onto 100 and prepare for an unforgettable drive.

Route 100 goes north past little mills and up through the ravine of the headwaters of the White River. It traces its way through the Granville Gulf and past lovely Moss Glen Falls (parking on the left, just beyond the Falls). Ten miles further, Route 100 is joined by the road from snow-covered Lincoln Gap on the left.

Now you're back to the summer route (page 42) and the drive east over Roxbury Mountain—if the weather is friendly, that is. If there's a doubt, better check in Warren before you go further. After all, you're in Vermont.

Smugglers Notch Loop. Another route, popular with visitor and Vermonter alike, is the twisting roadway across the spine of the mountains through Smugglers Notch near Jeffersonville. It's an exhilarating trip in summer but in winter? You've got to go around—although you'll still see miles of impressive mountains.

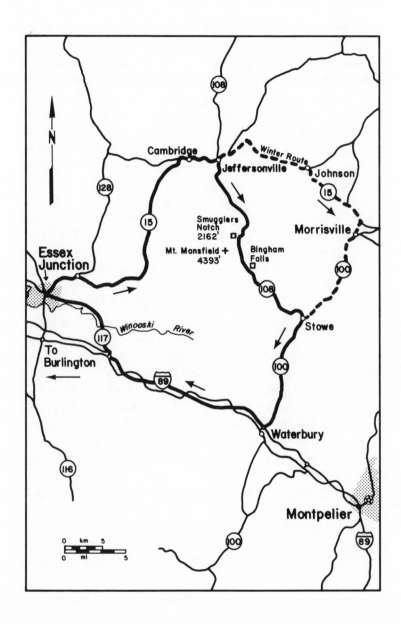

Begin your two-hour tour at Essex Junction, east of Burlington. Follow Route 15 east and north to Cambridge. Look for wildlife along this route. I've seen foxes, porcupines, and on one occasion I rearranged the contents of our car's trunk with an unscheduled S-turn around a sauntering skunk.

It's three miles from Cambridge to Jeffersonville. Turn right (south) off Route 15 at Jeffersonville and begin the climb on Vermont 108 toward Smugglers Notch—if it's summer. In winter, make a wider circle, continuing on Route 15 through the hilly town of Johnson with its state college. Stay on 15 to Morrisville, then south (right) on Route 100 to Stowe. This route misses Smugglers Notch, but the nearby mountains are grand just the same.

Smugglers Notch, which is closed all winter, is precipitous and winding, with arresting views of cliffs and peaks. Pull off into the parking area and look high in the rocks for the Old Smuggler's face. There's also the singing bird, plus the hunter and his dog. On a recent visit there we were entranced for an hour by the exploits of four rock climbers. The fearless four waved to their rapt audience when they reached the cliff top— and were rewarded by a chorus of auto horns.

If you try that steep road and those hairpin turns, better go in a plain automobile. The road is not for trailers or hefty campers. We once watched, spellbound, as a big tour bus shoehorned its way out of one jam and into another. Luckily the driver had power steering to help him out or the place would have been closed all summer, too.

The Smugglers Notch road (Route 108) leads south and downward past Bingham Falls (on your left; well worth the short walk to its cool waters) and past the toll road stretching eight miles to the ridges of Mt. Mansfield. Follow Route 108 to Stowe, where it joins Route 100. Continue south on 100 to Waterbury.

At Waterbury take Interstate 89 West, to Burlington. This

curves through jagged rock cuts and past rugged terrain. Indeed, the next fifteen miles is some of the most captivating scenery you'll encounter on any New England superhighway.

Take Exit 11 north off the Interstate to Route 117 and Essex Junction. You'll parallel the Winooski River much of the way to the five corners of the Junction. Then, if you have a few minutes go south (left) on Park Street two blocks to the little frame dwelling that houses the Discovery Museum.

This museum is a delightful place. The wooden carving of a bear invites visitors. Entering from the rear parking lot, you are encouraged to touch, to handle, to try your hand at gadgets and switches. Animals come and go: there's been Quilliam the porcupine, for instance, and Oscar the skunk. Namboo the boa constrictor has been enjoyed from a distance by thousands of adults—and on more intimate terms by fully as many kids who don't know they're supposed to be scared.

Nonprofit all the way, the museum is well worth the small price of admission. If your family is along, you'll get special rates, too.

There. We've enjoyed a few of the Green Mountains of Vermont—plus a few extras like a floating bridge and a hands-on museum. But combining them isn't as far-fetched as it might seem: after all, they're at each other's back door.

And now for another step—from mountains to woodlands. It's hard to tell where one stops and the other begins. Trees and shrubs grow wherever they can make a living, and so do the animals that depend on them. So you can never be sure what you'll encounter next, which makes almost any visit to the Vermont woodlands an adventure.

3

A Walk in the Woods

Leaving the mountains with their evergreens you come to the lower woodlands—the land of the hardwood trees. These are the ones that add so much color to the autumn scene just before they drop their leaves. Chief among them is the sugar maple, Vermont's offical state tree.

The fall complexion of the sugar maple can range from bronze through purple and flaming red to blazing orange and yellow. All these colors may be found in a single grove, on a single tree or—incredible as it may seem—a single leaf.

Maple leaves are usually borne in matched pairs along the twig. The twigs sprout in pairs along the stem, and so on. Such a two-by-two arrangement is known as opposite branching. With a few exceptions, most other Vermont trees have alternate branching, where single buds are staggered, right and left, at intervals.

The veins or ribs of a maple leaf spread out like the fingers of your hand. It is called, sensibly enough, palmately veined. To tell a sugar maple leaf from that of its red maple cousin, think of the "u" in sugar. The clefts, or sinuses, between the

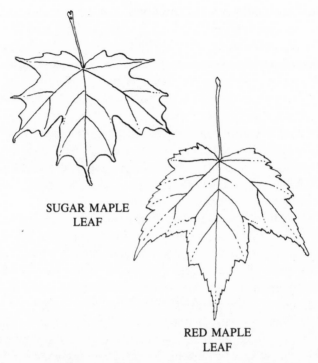

SUGAR MAPLE
LEAF

RED MAPLE
LEAF

lobes of the sugar maple leaf are "U" shaped. Those of the red species are more nearly "V" shaped: "V" for vermilion, I guess, to stretch a point.

Red maples provide plenty of fall color of their own. They color the winter scene a bit as well, with large, globular red buds. Indeed, look at a twig from almost any tree species, summer or winter. Even when leaves are present, next year's buds are there too. They can act as spares if needed after a late killing frost or drought. Otherwise they're waiting long months, to be awakened next spring. The sugar maple bud is smaller, more pointed, and brownish than its red maple cousin.

You can get sap and syrup from either species of maple—or, for that matter, from many trees in the spring. My sister and

I once cooked down a gallon of butternut sap. I guess we figured if butternuts were tasty the syrup would be, too. We got syrup all right—thick and dark and looking as if it belonged on somebody's driveway. After one taste we recycled it.

The only other common tree species to share the maples' opposite branching habit is the American ash. It often shares the same woodland, too. Ash has compound leaves: half a dozen paired leaflets arranged along a central supporting rib. White ash, as it's often called, may be the tallest deciduous tree in the forest. It makes a fine fire and can often be coaxed to burn even when green. Each ash seed has a little wing that makes it whirl like a helicopter as it falls.

The veins of ash leaves are similar in appearance to a feather. The Latin word for feather, *pinna*, forms the basis for the name of this type of growth: pinnate venation. Most Vermont hardwoods have pinnately veined leaves—except the palmately veined maples, of course, and a few others.

Sharing the zone of tallest trees, or overstory, are birch and beech, with an occasional black cherry. White birch's papery outer bark makes good emergency kindling; it will light even in the rain. Wisps of yellow birch bark, glistening golden bronze in color, will do the same. Just the wisps, by the way. To pull thick bark strips can kill a birch.

I demonstrate this easy-lightability to my youthful audiences when I take campers for nature hikes. They soberly commit it to memory, although I doubt they'll ever need the knowledge—roughing it smoothly, so to speak, with today's instant-burn fuels and camp stoves. They also love to smell and chew yellow birch's wintergreen-flavored twigs.

It's fun to identify the "initial tree": the American beech, with its smooth gray bark just waiting for a kid with a jackknife. The large, toothed leaves are reluctant to leave the tree in fall; some may stay all winter. Sugar maple leaves have this habit, as well.

Beech nuts in their bristly little burrs are triangular in appearance, like a pyramid. Green or ripe, they're a favorite wildlife food. On old trees look for ascending crescents of claw marks made by a black bear as it scooted up the trunk for a beech-nut feast.

BEAR CLAW MARKS ON BEECH

Black cherry trees are often beset with a multitude of troubles. So common is the black knot disease, for instance, that it's a good identification mark. It creates bumps and bulges on the twigs, making them grow backwards, sideways or in other unpredictable directions. Aphids attack the shiny leaves, causing them to curl. Galls shaped like warts or miniature bird nests or tiny elfin fingers grow from the leaf surface.

Sniff a broken cherry twig; it smells of bitter almond. That's the aroma of minute traces of cyanide. There's not enough to

51

hurt you but it's potentially harmful in quantity. It gets concentrated after the foliage is injured; a friend of mine lost a prize ram after it ate wilted cherry brush. Veterinarians often carry "cyanide antidote" as part of their kit during the summer months.

The fruit of the black cherry, also called rum cherry, is dark, shiny, and edible. Hanging in the late summer sun it may ferment. I've seen tipsy robins groggily clinging to a limb and teetering precariously as they stretched for one more taste of the forbidden fruit.

A tree's "fruit," by the way, can include nuts and seeds as well as juicy items such as cherries and apples. The fruit of oaks, for instance, can be a sure way to identify these trees. It's hard to mistake an acorn. Vermont oaks are usually found at lower elevations or in places a bit sheltered from our fiercest weather. You'll find them along roads of the Connecticut and Champlain valleys, for instance. The lobed leaves are distinctive, with white oak having rounded lobes while those of the red oak are more angular, ending in a sharp little point.

Oaks often grow in company with the shagbark hickory tree. The hickory's distinctive bark is attached in great jagged flakes that curve away from the trunk in such a way as to defy climbing. Then, should you somehow climb up, there's another problem: how to get down again. The bark is just as unforgiving in one direction as in the other.

A good frost splits hickory nuts from their thick, four-parted husks. Then you've got to hurry. The squirrels will take every one they can find. Hickory leaves are compound, like ash leaves. The lumber is used, as is ash, for tool handles, sports equipment and in other places where a strong, springy wood is needed.

The finest axe with the best handle may come to grief when up against the wood of hardhack, or ironwood. This small tree is apparently happy to dwell in the shade of its larger neighbors, making up for its size with a wood of incredible hardness. I once took a swing at a hardhack with a new scout axe and chipped a beautiful halfmoon of metal the size of an eggshell out of the blade.

As a general rule, the harder the wood the better it is as fuel. Tough woods like hardhack, oak, and sugar maple burn with a steady flame and keep well as glowing logs without burning out. Seasoned apple is a fine fuel as well, while the softer species like gray birch and poplar produce an enthusiastic flame but soon burn to ashes.

Hardhack bark, by the way, is shredded in appearance. The individual bark scales have a squared-off look. Its leaves have many small teeth along the margin. A seed-bearing structure that looks like a papery pine cone resembles the fruit of the hop vine. This gives the tree another name, hop hornbeam.

You'll find other trees in special places: slender-leaved willows along streams, or an occasional butternut hanging on from better days when this woodland was a field. Its compound leaves spring alternately from stout twigs. These twigs, hollowed of their dark brown pith, make dandy peashooters for small boys in school. Or so I've been told.

Since most of our forests have grown up from cutover land, you'll find remnants of the past among the trees and shrubs. Wild apples, for instance, may grow deep in the woods—the progeny of a discarded apple core, perhaps, when someone went to get the cows in what was then a pasture. Squirrels and chipmunks also carry apples from place to place. Deer and bears swallow the seeds and later pass them out unharmed in their droppings. Hence the sight of a woodland apple tree is, in effect, a peek into history.

If you stray from some woodland trail you may learn more than you wish about stumblebush. Also called hobblebush, or witch hobble, it has heart-shaped opposite leaves and clusters of small white flowers in spring. Its winter buds seem made of two tiny, hairy, cinnamon-colored leaves. The "hobble" part comes from the tendency of the branch tips to root where they touch the ground. The arch thus formed is a delightful trap for your unwary foot.

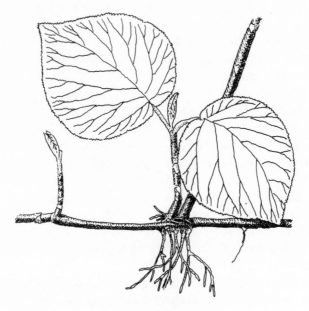

WITCH HOBBLE

A more friendly little plant is the dwarf dogwood. Just a few inches tall, it's related to the popular spring-flowering tree found south of our region. Look for its showy, four-parted white blossoms topping a whorl of six leaves. Those blossoms mature into a tight scarlet cluster—hence its common name, bunchberry. I've seen solid bunchberry mats half the size of a tennis court— as pretty as a Christmas scene, with red fruit awaiting the visit of a ruffed grouse or a woodland rodent.

Solid mats of foliage are also quite typical of the common

wood sorrel or oxalis. Its three-parted leaves look like a little Irish shamrock. If you're thirsty, chew a few of its leaves; they taste like lemonade. This starts your saliva flowing—and there goes your thirst.

WOOD SORREL

Sorrel is able to grow in the shade of tall trees. Not so with many small plants, however—yet they may live deep in the woods. They get around such a contradiction by a simple arrangement: they grow and bloom before the trees put out their leaves in the spring.

Three such early risers are bloodroot, hepatica, and the spring beauty. Bloodroot's golden-centered white flower arises from within the embrace of its curled leaf. The juice of its root was used by Indians as a dye and as red war paint. Hepatica's lavender or whitish flowers arise on single, hairy stems above three-lobed leaves. The several light pink flowers of spring beauty have dark pink stripes. They rise on a single stalk above a pair of twinned, slender leaves halfway up that same stalk.

Spring beauty's underground tubers remind us of little sweet potatoes; they taste a bit like them, too. Luckily, the little plant sometimes carpets acres of woodland all by itself, so it'll usually survive the attention of natural food buffs.

One of the most readily identified plants is the dogtooth violet, or trout lily. It bears the latter name for the brown mottling on its two thickened green leaves, suggestive of the colors of a trout. Its single yellow lilylike bloom rises on a solitary stem from these leaves at ground level.

On your woodland walk look for the jack-in-the-pulpit. Its green hood, streaked with brown, hangs over the central floral parts like an awning over a little preacher ("Jack"). Later that central section matures to a cluster of bright red berries.

The red trillium or wakerobin, with three-parted leaves and flower, is given the descriptive name "stinkpot" by my neighbors for the decaying odor of its liver-colored blooms. It's pollinated by carrion flies, just as bees pollinate sweeter flowers. The berry is bright red, as are those of the less feisty white species and the rare pink and white painted trillium.

Another red blossom is the pink ladyslipper, or moccasin flower. It's a treat to discover this true orchid of our cool woodlands. The red-veined blossom atop a bare stalk rises above a pair of basal leaves at ground level. The blossom is shaped like a pouch—or, I suppose, like the toe of a slipper.

The two or three large, flat green leaves of Clintonia, common over many a woodland, resemble the more papery leaves of the ladyslipper. The blossom is quite different, however: three or more yellow flowers on a single stem. Later, its berries are a deep blue. The intensity of its color makes this foot-high little lily—also known as bluebeads—one of the forest's most striking plants.

Scattered among all these plants you'll usually find several kinds of mosses. Some of them form dense rounded clumps while others are loose and scraggly. Many are tricky to tell apart, but the haircap moss has distinctive little stalks, each topped by a tiny capsule. The tip of the capsule is shed when ripe, exposing a structure like a miniature saltshaker. Tap it, watch a little cloud of spores fly out—and you've helped increase the moss population.

One familiar growth is not a moss at all, although it looks like it. This is the so-called reindeer moss—actually a member of the group of leathery plants known as lichens. Looking like a tiny, gray, much-branched tree, the three-inch reindeer moss may occur in clumps scattered in a forest opening as if tossed about by the handful. Farther north it is an important food source for deer and caribou. I tried it once on a camping cookout as a boy scout, and I suppose it might make an emergency stew. Otherwise I'll leave it to the caribou.

Lichens are cosmopolitan little beings, by the way. Various members of their far-flung tribe grow as greenish-gray crusts on rocks and exposed surfaces all over the world. Composed of bits of algae held in a fungus network, these little self-contained gardens often decorate logs and stumps in the forest. Many a treetrunk carries spots and patches of lichens—sometimes as far up as the eye can see.

Vermont woodlands are rich in ferns. You may readily spot the interrupted fern because the greenery of some of its fronds is interrupted part way up the stalk by brownish, spore-bearing organs. Its relative, the cinnamon fern, has a central spore-bearing frond covered with brownish fluff. The hummingbird often gathers this wispy material for its golfball-sized nest.

Hay-scented or boulder ferns form solid stands of light yellowish-green on a partly open slope. Like soldiers in formation, they arrange themselves so each is broadside to the available light. Then, as the day advances, they slowly turn to follow the course of the sun through the sky.

Most individual of all, perhaps, is the Christmas fern. Sturdily built and deep green in color, it remains very much alive

INTERRUPTED FERN

beneath the winter snow. It's Christmasy in summer, too: each little leaflet along the stem is shaped like a tiny yuletide stocking—heel, toe, and all.

Distantly related to ferns are the clubmosses or running pines. Seldom more than a few inches high, they run along the ground by means of horizontal stems that produce a little green tree-like structure every few inches. This trailing habit made them popular for Christmas wreaths until relative scarcity put them on the protected list.

In the early days of the camera, a product of clubmoss was part of the photographer's stock in trade. Tiny dustlike spores from small cones on the plants are highly inflammable, and were ignited for flash powder. They've even been used for fireworks.

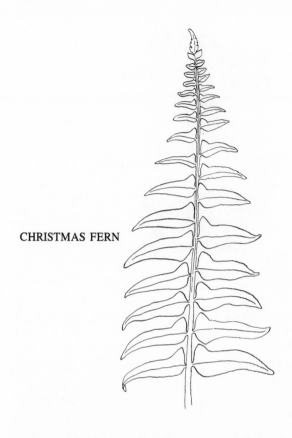

CHRISTMAS FERN

    Spores are also the standard means of reproduction of those interesting little creations known as mushrooms. Easy to spot are the familiar leathery bracket fungi on the trunks of trees. These make fine sketch pads; on their snowy underside you can scratch pictures or names with a stick. When fresh they'll show the bruise mark of a fingerprint, but after drying on a shelf, they'll last for years.

    My mother wrote on a bracket fungus during one of our woodland jaunts half a century ago. Today it's a priceless reminder of my boyhood days. An acquaintance of mine sometimes finds

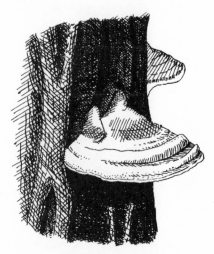

BRACKET FUNGUS

a conch, as it is also called, when visiting some friend in the country—and then gives it back, suitably inscribed with autograph and doodles, at Christmas time.

The fleshy fungi can be bewildering in color and variety. People frequently ask how to tell the edible from unfriendly ones, and I admit there's no sure way. Unfortunately, some of the worst actors taste just fine. Supposedly an unwholesome mushroom will darken a silver spoon if cooked with it, but so will an egg. It doesn't even help to observe what mushrooms are eaten by animals, either—some wild creatures seem to have a digestion like a cement mixer.

Edible or not, here are a few fungi you might meet along the way. We'll generally ignore their gastronomical qualities. Almost all mushrooms, like the conchs on trees, gain nourishment from dead or decaying plant material. Hence you'll often find them around an extinct tree or buried log.

One familiar mushroom group is known as the puffballs. Many a woodland stump sports a cluster of marble-sized mushrooms—white or honeycolored on the outside and snowy within. Cut one open. If the interior is completely homogeneous and mealy throughout, chances are you're in the presence of good, wholesome puffballs.

Since many other mushrooms begin life as rounded little buttons, however, you've got to be certain there are no hidden gills or stems or other parts. The best way, if you're not sure, is just to admire them—or wait until they turn brown and powdery inside. Then you can have the fun of squeezing them so little clouds of spores erupt from a hole in the top. Old timers have long used these spores as a sort of snuff to stop nosebleeds.

There are various edible puffballs: tiny, white, prickly-looking ones in a woodland clearing and the familiar open field giants that may weigh ten pounds or more. The leather-skinned species with a black interior is generally listed as inedible—not surprising for something with all the appeal of an overcooked golf ball.

PUFFBALL

Puffballs, of course, do not have gills. Neither do the species known as boletes—shaped like a conventional mushroom but with a spongy underside made of thousands of tiny tubes. These tubes open on the lower surface as little pores. The tops of various boletes resemble, among other things, a well-baked muffin, an oversized egg yolk and a chunk of fresh liver. The sensitive boletus apparently has its own ideas as to a color scheme. When its light-colored flesh is wounded, it turns a startling deep blue.

The gilled species includes dozens of kinds. They range from oyster mushrooms that grow up a tree trunk like their marine namesakes clinging to a harbor piling to the tawny ink caps that subside into a sloppy black mess overnight.

There is even a mushroom that glows in the dark. It is the orange colored Jack-o-Lantern, occasionally found on rotting wood. Indeed, one of the phosphorescent woods known as foxfire may contain the fungal threads of this species.

The mushroom that makes people wary is one of the most handsome of all, the amanita. Actually there are several species, but two of the worst actors are the fly amanita and the

OYSTER MUSHROOM

death angel. Both these species have a collar or ring around the stem plus a volva or "death cup" around a swollen base.

The fly amanita is orange or yellow on top, usually sprinkled with whitish scales. The ground below may be littered with insects that came for a snack and got a surprise. The death angel is almost uniformly smooth and white. Interestingly, squirrels sometimes cache amanitas in the fork of a limb, where they dry in the sun for weeks. This apparently makes them edible— for squirrels, at least.

Squirrels, by the way, are not always the vegetarians we may suppose them to be. As it explores the treetops for cones and tender buds, the red squirrel may come upon a bird nest or a moth cocoon. The feisty little rodent with the white underbelly and expressive tail makes short work of its find—and races off to more mischief. Other squirrels are opportunists, too. The gray squirrel may forsake its diet of nuts and acorns when it comes across a nest of eggs or even young birds.

The same is true of the flying squirrel—that nocturnal creature with the silky fur, large eyes, and wrist-to-ankle flaps that allow it to glide, spread-eagled, from one tree to the next. As with most squirrels, the flying squirrel has an outsized dose of curiosity. Scratch your fingernails gently on the bark of a likely hollow tree in the forest. My father once showed me how to do this—and immediately five pairs of liquid-dark eyes surveyed us soberly from a knothole twenty feet above our heads.

That striped ground squirrel, the chipmunk, lives in an earthen tunnel or beneath a rock. The little rodent is an incurable hoarder, packing away seeds and wild cherry pits and the winged samaras of maple (with wings clipped) as fast as it can cram them into its capacious cheeks. Then it whisks them off to an underground vault. Sometimes it filches the eggs from a bird nest and stores them, too. I am convinced the only thing that keeps chipmunks from making off with half the edibles in Vermont is one little detail: the chipmunks sleep most of the winter.

CHIPMUNK

One small rodent may catch your attention even if all you
do is hear it. The deer mouse makes an astonishing racket sometimes as it pokes through the leaves for nuts and seeds. If you
see it, the large dark eyes, great paper-thin ears, and snowy
underside make it one of nature's most appealing creatures—
until it avails itself of the hospitality of your woodland cabin.
Then it helpfully fills your shoes, the corner of a drawer, and
any other handy container with seeds. I've even known the
whitefoot, as it's often called, to take up a weekend abode in
the trunk of a vacationist's car.

Both cabin and car may become objects of great interest to
that myopic meanderer, the porcupine. Anything that bears a
trace of salt from sweaty hands or salted winter roads engages
the quill pig's complete attention. Its flinty incisors may anni-
hilate an axe handle. It gnaws automobile tires. One day thir-

teen campers showed up at our door. A porky had helpfully eaten through the brake lines of their van where they'd parked it for an overnight hike.

Although a black bear or even a mountain lion will respectfully back away from a porky, there is little for us humans to fear. A porcupine cannot throw its quills. In its nearsighted way, it bumbles through life summer and winter, placidly seeking a stomach full of twigs and flowers and leaves and bark. Sometimes it'll stay in a tasty tree for a week—blizzards, storms, and all.

Like the porky, the snowshoe hare is active all winter. Also called the varying hare, it turns from brown to white in snow season. Its feet grow fluffy snowshoes, allowing it to bound over the deepest drifts. This it may do all night with the same exuberance it has in summer. Result: a bewildering maze of tracks that may defy unraveling.

Hares and rabbits (the smaller cottontail rabbit is more a creature of meadow and pasture than of woodland) eat the twigs of seedling trees and brambles and other shrubs in winter. Often

DEER MOUSE

SNOWSHOE HARE

they stand on their hind legs and pull the branches down within reach so the twigs look as if lopped off by a gigantic rabbit the size of a deer.

Deer chew on twigs and branches, too, but their feeding technique is different. Deer have no upper front teeth, so they break off twigs and stems by a combination of tongue, upper palate, and a twist of the head. Rabbits (and their look-alike but unrelated neighbors, the rodents) tilt the head sideways so those chisel teeth can get a good grip. Hence if you see a twig cut on a slant it's probably the work of rabbit or rodent. If it's ragged and frayed it was most likely done by a deer—or by some farmer's wayward cow. Cows and sheep and goats could use a set of uppers, too.

Look for the whitetail deer at a forest border at dusk. Deer are quite at home in the deep woods, but there is little food there. As with many animals, they often prefer woodland clearings or the junction of forested land and meadow. Here they enjoy the so-called edge effect where trees and shrubs and grassland meet. Hence an animal has everything within a few leaps of safety.

Incidentally, you and I like the edge effect, too. We prefer the corner lot, a beachfront, an apartment with a view—in other words, as much variety as possible. There's a little of the country in all of us, I guess, even in the city.

You cannot consider the Vermont woods very long without thinking of the black bear. Items on a bear's agenda may include pulling rotting logs apart from grubs or digging up half the forest for a chipmunk who's scarcely flattered by all the attention. And nearly every Vermonter seems to know somebody who accidentally picked wild berries in the same patch as a bear— until both corrected the mistake at full speed and in opposite directions.

There's little danger from a black bear in the Vermont woods, except to your peace of mind if you fancy one lurking nearby. Make plenty of noise if you suffer from ursophobia; the natural aversion of *Ursus* to humans will do the rest.

With the bear's diminutive cousin, the raccoon, it is another story. Raccoons get along quite well in the presence of people, as thousands of upset garbage cans will attest. To the ringtailed little creature nearly anything is edible until proven otherwise.

Go ahead. Hang your provisions from a tree limb somewhat removed from your sleep quarters if you're camping—you'll probably rest better. But don't be surprised at what you find in the morning. The black-masked burglar has either pulled the food up within reach or it has slid down the rope to sample the whole affair.

Cosmopolitan taste serves the skunk well, too. Luckily the slow-going creature cannot climb. A gas attack from the tree-tops would be terrible indeed. Anything at altitude zero, however, from soil-inhabiting grubs to the eggs of ground-nesting birds may be duly consumed by the placid little peacemaker.

Luckily, as with raccoon and bear, the skunk retires in the fall. Thus the winter woods are fraught with fewer perils—which, I suppose, may help explain the popularity of cross-country skiing.

The skunk's little cousin, the weasel, seems made of springs and rubber bands. Few creatures are more alert. A weasel can see the flash of a gun and dodge the bullet. Leaf-brown in summer, it dons a coat of white in winter—except for black nose, eyes, and tip of tail. Virtually unshakeable in pursuit of its prey, following it down into burrows and through the densest thickets, the implacable nemesis was aptly named years ago by nature writer Thornton W. Burgess: Shadow the Weasel.

One wild cat and two wild dogs also keep the nibblers and gnawers in balance. The cat is that stump-tailed cousin of the common tabby, the bobcat. It may reach nearly twice the size of its domestic relative, but for all its fearsome reputation, the wildcat doesn't dine on vacationers. It would rather have birds, rabbits, and similar prey.

The two wild dogs are the red fox and the eastern coyote.

The red fox, an attractive creature, is a bit larger than a big tomcat. Its black legs and feet contrast with its rusty-red fur and white-tipped bushy tail. It almost seems to glide as it races across a woodland clearing, and it's a study in concentration as it gathers for a pounce on a mouse.

Both sexes care for the fox pups. If an enemy approaches

RED FOX

their hillside den, the parents may attempt to lure it away. A friend of mine happened across a fox household near an old stone wall. "That vixen barked and whined and limped as if she had the galloping epizootic," Don Brown told me. "She put on such an act that the pups came back out of the hole and sat bolt upright to watch—and that blew the whole secret, right there."

Three times the size of the ten-pound fox, the eastern coyote often travels in small family groups. A pack of coyotes tuning up with yipping bark may stir up an entire valley of farm dogs. Coyotes are not the slightest threat to humans, unless you count the sleepless hours before the dogs cease the racket—whereupon the coyotes start them up again.

We've already met the shrews, up on the mountain. They're down here, too—several species, all of them hungry and all of them fearless. Once our phlegmatic old horse was stampeded by a shrew. Flash had stumbled onto its nest, and the outraged creature put him into a panic.

Many birds roost and nest high enough to be safe from a shrew. The irascible Tom Thumb snoops all over but seldom climbs. A ground nester like the ruffed grouse or partridge, however, may occasionally lose some of her dozen eggs at the base of a tree or up against a fallen log. A few of the babies themselves would probably escape; the precocious little chicks can run and hide within hours after hatching.

One of the forest's impressive performances is that of a mother grouse in defense of her young. Wing drooping, one leg trailing as if broken, the mottled brown bird with the fan-shaped tail flutters just ahead of the enemy—hissing and crying as if horribly wounded. Farther and farther she goes until she has safely enticed her foe from danger. Then, as if by a miracle, she gets better and flies triumphantly away on thundering wings.

Seldom seen but often heard is the drumming ritual of the male ruffed grouse. Mounting a favorite fallen log, the grouse

"WOUNDED" GROUSE

beats its wings in an ever-increasing tempo, making an accelerating thumping sound that ends in a muffled flurry. Grouse have been known to attack a farm tractor in the woods, perhaps to drive away this snorting rival.

While you may find the grouse in almost any forest, the wild turkey often prefers woods with abundant nuts and acorns. These become grist for its energetic little mill. This mill is a muscular gizzard, well able to cope with the hard shells of nuts and seeds.

The turkey can also thrive on the gleaning of corn and oats and other crops left behind after fall harvest. I've seen flocks of a dozen or more in corn fields near Rupert, Dorset, Panton, and Bristol—and in some areas of the Connecticut River valley as well.

A woodland walk can stir up a flock of chickadees. These companionable birds may accompany you quite a distance. As they go they ostensibly inspect twigs and leaves for insects—but quite likely they're really inspecting you.

The chickadees' cousins, the black and white nuthatches, run headfirst down the trunk of a tree, searching for food in this inverted position. This has given them the name of upside-downs or, as one neighbor lady calls them, assups. "But that's all one word," she hastily assured me.

The upper branches come under the attention of birds by the score—the robin-sized hairy woodpecker, for instance, and the smaller downy woodpecker. You'll often see rows of holes in regular order around a trunk or limb: the work of the yellow-bellied sapsucker. This large woodpecker with red forehead (plus red throat on the male) drills those holes to return later to feed on the resultant sap plus insects attracted by the sweet liquid.

Largest of all, the pileated woodpecker makes long rectangular holes in the sides of decaying stubs. The bird itself is impressive: as big as a crow, with a bright red cap, or pileum.

People misunderstand the work of this bird in its search for carpenter ants and other insects. Once I asked a lady if she had seen the woodpecker that had hollowed out a six-foot furrow in the dying maple on her lawn. "Yep," she said laconically, "but we took care of him."

Other treetop feeders include the warblers, which may be told by their bright colors, insistent songs, and almost constant motion. Thus they contrast with the more sedate olive-and-white vireos, the striped or somber-colored sparrows, and the brownish thrushes. These latter birds search for food on the forest floor or sing their exquisite flutelike songs from a quiet perch on limb or shrub.

Vermont's state bird, the hermit thrush, has a leaf-brown back and a rusty tail. It frequently lowers the tail quickly and then slowly raises it to normal position. Its song, often heard in late

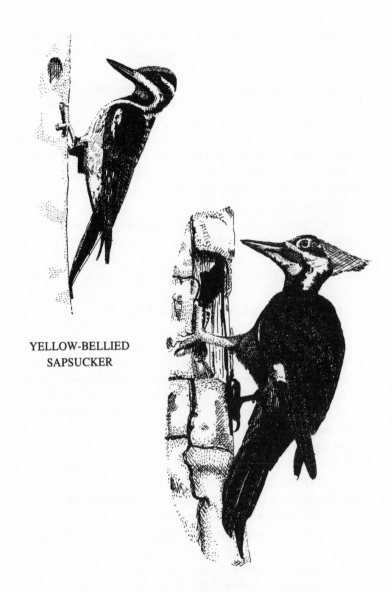

YELLOW-BELLIED
SAPSUCKER

PILEATED WOODPECKER

afternoon, is a single low note followed by half a dozen higher-pitched rising notes. The series is repeated eight to ten times a minute, each time in a different key.

At least two birds of prey roam the forest—the goshawk and the great horned owl. The gray goshawk's short, rounded wings and long tail allow it to maneuver through the trees after birds as large as the ruffed grouse. The owl's keen eyes and acute hearing plus its silent flight enable it to strike a bird or small mammal on the darkest night. One of its favorite targets is the skunk. Such a preference doubtless tells something about the owl's sense of smell.

Once I heard of an owl that flew off with a gentleman's hat. It might have been a coonskin cap, I suppose—or maybe, under even less happy circumstances, a toupee. And famed bird photographer Eric Hosking lost an eye to an owl that struck at its gleam in the dusk. Beyond such hazards, however, the birds of prey can scarcely be considered a threat to life and limb—of people, at least.

Nor is there any more danger in another group of creatures fully as harmless, yet the cause of much needless fear and apprehension. They are the victims of slander and unfriendly public relations: the snakes. These inoffensive beings, supposedly lurking behind every bush, are as much a part of Vermont as mountains and maple trees.

Our poisonous snakes add up to exactly one: the timber rattlesnake. Native to our entire northeast, the rattler has its last Vermont retreat in a few west central rocky areas near the New York border. Even there it is so rare that the sighting of a single rattler often brings about a small war until it is vanquished. Apparently we want to get out in the country but not down to earth.

The other woodland snakes, the red-bellied, the ringnecked, and the little brown snake, are small and secretive. They are not much larger than a pencil, live under rocks and logs, feed on worms and insects, and could be defeated by anybody's puppy.

The wood turtle, despite its name, is more of brushland and little streams than of the forest. This peaceful eight-inch reptile with brick-red body parts and yellow-black lower shell is quietly losing its contest with civilization. It needs clear woodland streams, unsilted by so-called improvements, for its courtship. The female lays her eggs in open sandy areas—which, unfortunately, are abundant along roadsides. Such a venture for the turtle is often a one-way trip. Incidentally, if you wish to rescue a turtle crossing a road, place it on the side toward which it was heading. It's no use trying to put it back where it came from—it'll just turn around and head for the road again. A turtle, apparently, has a one-track mind.

Amazingly abundant but almost unknown to a casual visitor are the amphibians—the frogs and toads and salamanders. Marc DesMeules, biologist with the Nature Conservancy in Montpelier, points out they may actually outweigh the birds and small mammals in some forests. Yet they are so quiet and shy—except during the spring mating season—that we seldom see even one on a woodland walk.

Look under rotting logs or flat stones for the little red-backed salamander. About the size of an earthworm, it is colored as its name implies, or it may be a somber leaden hue. Its cousin the brook salamander is found under stones washed by forest streams. When discovered, it dashes about like a little fish.

Take a walk after a rain; you'll probably find yourself in the company of the little red eft. This plodding rain lizard is no lizard at all but the juvenile stage of the common yellow-bellied pond salamander or newt. It may be a landlubber for years, coming out on back-country roads and wandering all through the woods. Apparently its color warns of its inedibility; I've seen a cat pounce on a red eft and just as suddenly fling it aside.

Spotted salamanders, their bluish-black uppersides bearing

round yellow spots, usually hide during the day. Occasionally they wander into someone's cellar, which means my phone may ring. Then I spend the next few minutes reassuring some fearful family as to the harmlessness of "this *Thing* that's as big as a hot dog and *must* be poisonous!"

Impressive, too, are the wood frog and spring peeper—in the vocal department, that is. Resounding from a pond that may still have ice at one end, a wood frog's mating chorus sounds like a flock of ducks. The piercing whistles of the peeper are like the chirps of some kind of bird.

Sometimes the peeper reminisces, so to speak, from a low tree or shrub in summer, but the inch-long singer is almost invisible. Brown in color with a dark "X" on the back, it closely matches its surroundings.

Twice the peeper's size, the wood frog inhabits the forest floor. The long leaps of this black-masked brown creature carry it well out of the way of your advancing footsteps. If we could do as well for our size, we'd clear a tennis court, end-to-end, in a single bound.

Standard fare for frogs and salamanders is the population of insects and similar creatures abounding in our Vermont countryside. In spring, especially, you wish those amphibians all the luck as new-hatched biting insects head for your epidermis. Black flies are there to welcome you, along with punkies or no-see-ums, and mosquitoes. Such hazards are seasonal, however, and as spring fades their numbers decrease.

The spotted-winged or deer fly, on the other hand, may remain painfully in evidence all summer. It circles around your head with a maddening buzz. The trouble is not in the buzz, however, but in when it stops.

In spite of such pesky creatures, most insect species are either harmless or actually beneficial. We're not bothered with termites in Vermont, but even these blind little sawdust makers have a vital role in the reprocessing of downed trees. A few unsavory actors such as the gypsy moth and forest tent caterpillar give a bad name to the whole insect group.

To many people the best thing for a swift-running beetle is to squash it. Actually, such active creatures are usually predatory on other insects. After all, leaves and trees and edible plants cannot get away, so there's no need for haste for the leaf-chomping insects. Therefore when you blot out a speeding beetle's life the rest of the insect world rejoices.

Big black carpenter ants make galleries in decaying logs. The condominiums of mound-building ants may be knee high and three feet in diameter. There are little yellow ants, brown ants, even red-and-black ants. You'll find them in all sorts of situations. But then, as any picnic-goer knows, ants are everywhere.

You can spot some marvelous examples of protective shape and color among those insects. Touch a measuring worm on a tree; it sticks out stiffy and turns into a twig. Follow a brilliant blue satyr butterfly through a forest glade with your eye—and then lose it when it stops, folds its wings back-to-back, and becomes a brown leaf. Try to figure out which is sunlight and which is shadow when the spotted forester moth flies by. Wings flecked with black and white, it looks as if the sun-dappled forest floor has suddenly taken flight.

Yellow borders on brown wings mark the mourning cloak butterfly. It, too, resembles sunlight in fallen leaves. It sleeps most of the winter in a hollow tree or beneath a loose slab of bark. But it's a fitful sleeper; I've seen the mourning cloak abroad on a warm March day, drinking sap from a broken maple twig.

Even the cockroaches are easier to take in the woods. Pull apart a rotting log; you may find shiny brown wood roaches in company with boring grubs, bark beetles, and slender orange wireworm beetle larvae. The roaches scuttle in approved cockroach fashion, but they're not the type that stows aboard your

HIDDEN INSECT

pack and accompanies you home. They're wonderfully accomplished. Flip one on its back and its flexible legs frantically row it like a tiny boat to a spot where it can right itself.

Mites, ticks, and spiders are not insects, although they look like them. We're not much bothered with ticks in Vermont; our celebrated winters must be too much for them. Mites are mainly harmless, too, with the exception of one or two that cause mange in foxes and other animals. This leaves us with the spiders that, like the snakes, suffer from a bad press.

One interesting species is the wolf spider. It's so called

because it stalks its prey like its namesake rather than lurking in a web. It is large, hairy, and fleet of foot—all eight of them. You may come across a female burdened with her matronly duties—literally. Some wolf spider babies ride on their mother's back until ready to seek their own fortunes.

There are many woodland web-weavers but none that bother humans—unless you count those that helpfully string a strand of silk across your path at eye level. Apparently they do this by letting out a long thread. The wind catches the thread, carries it across the opening where it clings to a likely plant—and the deed is done. Of course the way to lessen the annoyance of spiderwebs in the face is to politely let someone else go first on the trail.

Centipedes? There are a number of species, prowling around in the leaf litter, and all harmless to humans. They're flat-bodied and segmented, with one pair of legs per segment. They catch insects and earthworms, overwhelming their prey with all those legs and a twisting, flexible body. Two poison fangs soon take the fight out of the victim.

CENTIPEDE

Less menacing, there in the world of the forest floor, are those peaceful animated tubes, the millipedes. They're also called thousand-legs because of their numerous appendages—actually two pairs of legs per segment. They are valuable scavengers, ridding the woods of decaying material. They also feed on mushrooms—plus other plant material, as many a gardener knows all too well.

MILLIPEDE

Joining the millipedes in cleanup duties are those slowpokes of the animal world, the slugs and snails. Slugs are essentially snails without a shell. They glide on a ribbon of mucus laid down as they travel. So delicately do these molluscs pick their way that a snail can easily traverse the length of a razor blade without getting cut.

There are many wood snails, but my favorite is the white-lipped species. It is half the size of a golf ball and named for the color of the opening of its brownish shell. To see its glistening two-inch body stretched out on a mossy stump as it quietly makes its way toward an undisclosed destination in a shady glen—to me, at least, this is the very soul of the Vermont woodland.

One time I chanced upon a spot where a black bear had left its droppings in a pile bigger than a softball. I wanted to take a picture, but it was a gray day, and I needed a flash for my camera. I returned the following day, carefully retracing my steps to the same spot.

The spot was there, all right, but the scene had changed. That bear's offering had apparently been gratefully received by every snail and slug in the forest. Mucus trails came from all directions. And there was what was left of my picture: a nondescript little heap that looked like the contents of somebody's teabag.

WHITE-LIPPED SNAIL

Where I'd Take You If I Could

It's difficult, really, to decide where we'd start out on a look at Vermont's forests. With three quarters of the state classified as woodland the trees are almost everywhere. Then, too, on any jaunt we'd also see items that would fit in other than wooded categories: swamps, mountains, lakes, fields.

It reminds me of my small grandson, Jared, who went for a short hike with me along a forest trail. "Now we are going on a nature walk," he remarked soberly. "Perhaps we will see some nature."

Rutland-Waitsfield-West Rutland Loop. Take that little chunk of virgin forest near Sherburne, for instance. Just north of the intersection of Routes U.S. 4 and Vermont 100, it's but five acres of the larger area known as Gifford Woods State Park. Yet in order to get there you cannot help but see plenty of Jared's "nature" of many kinds along the way.

Suppose you start at Rutland. It's a 130-mile loop, beginning at U.S. Route 4 east. Soon you're among the wooded hills of Mendon, climbing much of the time. Beech and birch and maple accompany you to Sherburne Pass, just about ten miles from the city traffic.

Pause here at the turnout where the combined Long and Appalachian Trails cross the road. Within a few hundred yards, if you venture along one well-marked pathway or another, you'll find most of the trees mentioned in this chapter. You'll see the pine and hemlock and spruce of the mountain chapter as well.

At winter's end those little pioneer spring flowers may welcome you. In autumn you can contemplate the fall foliage and try to realize that the colors were there all along, but masked by the now-fading green of chlorophyll.

Back on Route 4, continue about a mile east, dropping down

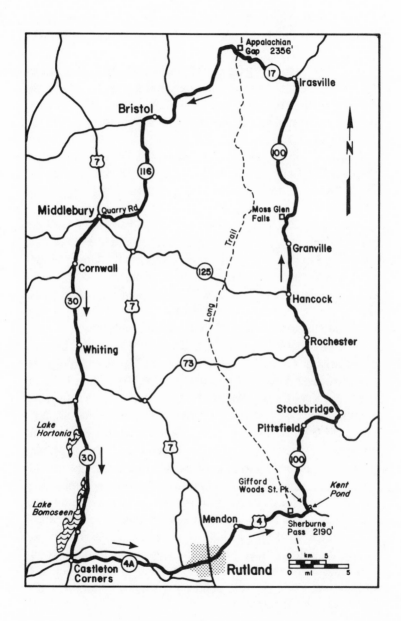

to Route 100. Turn left on 100 and pause a few minutes at my favorite Kent Pond on your right. Another quarter mile takes you to Gifford Woods.

The little stand of big trees is to your right. Here, in the quiet forest, the smoke from the campground across the road may filter through giant sugar maples, yellow birch, and American ash that were standing in that selfsame spot before our War of Independence.

Continue north on Route 100. Follow the Tweed River valley through Pittsfield with its long village green right beside the road. Drive on through Stockbridge to Rochester and more woodlands.

Just before Rochester, on the right, you can visit one of the Ranger Stations of the Green Mountain National Forest. One of the first in the nation, this forest straddles the Green Mountains along much of our state. It provides nearly 300,000 acres of back-country roads, trails, wilderness, and recreation areas. You'll find a friendly welcome at the station, along with free maps and literature, plus hints on local conditions.

From Rochester, continue on Route 100 through Hancock to the pristine Granville Gulf Reservation. Trees and rocks and a narrowing ravine lead you past lovely Moss Glen Falls on your left, a couple of miles north of Granville. (This is the road I promised in case you took the summer route in the last chapter.)

Continue on Route 100 to its intersection with Route 17 at Irasville. Turn left (west) on 17. Soon you climb through woods, past ski areas, and up to 2,356-foot Appalachian Gap (open all year). Here, at a wide parking place on the Gap, you may view more rolling forests to the north and west toward distant Lake Champlain. The Long Trail crosses the road here. Peg and I often take a short hike as long as we're in the neighborhood.

The road drops steeply from the Gap through more woods and tumbling little waterways. Look for deer and porcupines, plus beavers in a sizeable pond on the left a couple of miles after the road flattens out.

When Route 17 joins Route 116, turn left (south) onto this combined route. Soon you are in Bristol with its village green and bandstand—complete with summer band concerts on Wednesday nights.

A mile west of Bristol, turn left onto Route 116 at a crossroads. About nine miles south of this intersection, turn right on Quarry Road opposite a little white schoolhouse—now a community center. Nearly three miles further, make a sharp left turn onto Foote Street. A quarter mile south on this road is the Means Woods area with its little nature trail (left) plus the Battell Woods across the road.

Foote Street comes out on U.S. 7, where it's known as Schoolhouse Road. A sharp right (north) onto this highway takes you past the Middlebury Ranger Station of the Green Mountain National Forest (on your right in a mile or so, and well worth the visit), and on into Middlebury. Down along the town's Merchants Row and the bridge over Otter Creek, follow the signs to Route 30 south out of town.

Continue south on Route 30 through Cornwall and Whiting. You'll pass streams and ponds and swampland woods, past lovely lakes such as Hortonia and Bomoseen, and under the dual highway that is Route 4 (or onto it if you're in a hurry).

Turn left (east) just beyond this underpass onto Route 4A. Soon you're in Castleton with its State College, and on through more scenic wooded hills back to Rutland. As you come into Rutland, the main headquarters of the Green Mountain National Forest are upstairs in the Post Office building on West Street.

Gifford Woods to Sherburne Pass. For a closer look at some of the forest in the Rutland loop above, try this little hike. It takes less than two leisurely hours and stretches across almost every kind of territory in a mile and a half. It goes from tranquil pond to windy mountain pass; from deep forest to rocky ridge. Although it is uphill most of the way, there are a number of level spots at handy intervals.

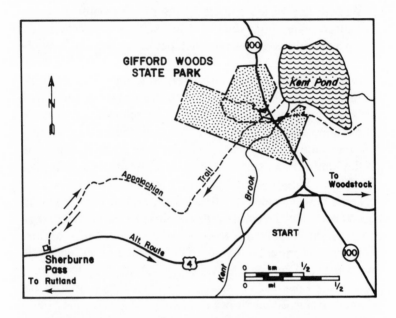

You begin near the junction of Routes U.S. 4 and Vermont
100, about twelve miles east of Rutland. This junction is about
two miles east of Sherburne Pass on Route 4. You'll come out
of the woods at this pass later, so if you feel like resting at the
end of your walk you may wish to have a car to pick you up
there.

Travel north on Route 100 about a quarter mile from its junction with Route 4. On the east (right) side of Route 100 at this
point is the public access area to Kent Pond. If you wish, you
may park the car here or go another few hundred feet and leave
the car by the Gifford Woods State Park headquarters.

The path you'll travel is a short segment of the Georgia-to-
Maine Appalachian Trail. It crosses Route 100 in an east-to-
west direction near the State Park entrance. First, however, walk
to the Kent Pond dam, a few hundred feet east of Route 100.

Notice the great trees in the nearby woods. These are a portion of one of the last stands of virgin timber in Vermont. There are no pathways through the trees but appreciative visitors are welcome. Many of these trees have grown up with our Green Mountain State. They were sturdy saplings even before Vermont's brief period as an independent republic from 1777 to 1791. Now the tall birches, sugar maples, and beeches stretch skyward with nary a limb for sixty feet and more.

At Kent dam, look over the surface of the pond for the splash of a feeding trout. In early fall many of those brookies, as they're called, fight their way up the stream that enters the pond near its southern end. It's worth parking at the access area and walking the few steps to watch these fish as they head upstream to spawn.

Backtrack along the trail through the forest and head west across Route 100. This will take you past Gifford Woods State Park headquarters. If you feel like a picnic, a stop at the restroom, or a visit to the playground, you may pay the modest entrance fee to use these facilities. Otherwise, as an Appalachian Trail hiker, merely continue along the campground access road to a spot near Campsite number 12. Here the trail heads up into the woods.

As you go through a grove of young ash, maple, and beech trees you'll cross a small, rocky trickle that may or may not be flowing, depending on the recent rainfall. You'll encounter this "sometimes stream," as Vermont poet Ann Day Heinzerling calls it, several times on your hike. You may also see streamside vegetation such as little nondescript liverworts, mosses on the moist stones, and a number of woodland ferns.

Springtime flowers in these woods include the speckled little trout lily, several types of violet, and windflowers (anemones) with their white blossoms. Later you'll find large patches of woodland asters with their many small white blooms, plus the indigo-colored fruit of bluebeads or clintonia, whose earlier yellow-green blossoms looked like half a dozen tiny lilies scattered along a single stalk.

The rocky trail ascends more steeply as you go along. Tree roots, exposed across the path by the tread of many feet, serve as natural stairs that allow good footing. Almost all the evergreen trees here are hemlocks with their lacy foliage and gracefully curving tips. You'll also see sizeable sugar maples, yellow birches, beech, and black cherry trees.

As you climb ever higher you begin to make the acquaintance of small red spruces along the way. Look for red squirrels among their boughs. You'll probably also see a flock of blue jays with their colorful coats and raucous screams.

The tumbled boulders around you tell of rock slides in the distant past. Now and again you'll see a chunk of white quartz, perhaps abandoned by the glacier that covered this area long ago. Trees, growing up and over these rocks, sometimes assume weird shapes as they make their way toward the light.

There have been a few white birches along the way. About a mile from your start you come upon several dozen of them scattered through the woods. Now and again, at this height, you'll see a small balsam fir standing erect in the woods like the little Christmas tree it is.

A few hundred yards past the white birches and just to the right of the trail is a massive boulder, resting squarely on an exposed rock platform. This glacial erratic, attesting to the power of the ice that brought it there, is capped by little polypody ferns. It also bears a few leathery bodies which look like fallen leaves resting on the rock. These are lichens, known as rock tripe, which supposedly make an emergency soup when boiled. I don't know; I've never been that hungry in the woods.

Shortly afterward the Appalachian Trail joins the Long Trail at a fork in the woods known as Maine Junction. The two continue as one pathway, dropping steeply through the forest. Soon you arrive at U.S. Route 4 at Sherburne Pass. Here you may retrace your steps to Route 100 and thus complete the round trip. Many hikers, unabashed by traffic, continue for an added mile-plus down the long hill of Route 4 past roadside flowers, hardwood forests, and a few white pines. A turn left (north) onto Route 100 brings you back to your start. Thus, you've completed the last side of a triangle, covering about three miles in the process.

Manchester-Londonderry Loop. Another, much shorter, tour (about forty miles) begins at Manchester Center. Drive east on Routes 30 and 11 to the Ranger Station of the Green Mountain National Forest. About two miles out of town and on your right, this station has many facilities: books, photos, aerial maps, and plenty of help from the staff.

When Routes 11 and 30 divide, follow Route 11 straight ahead

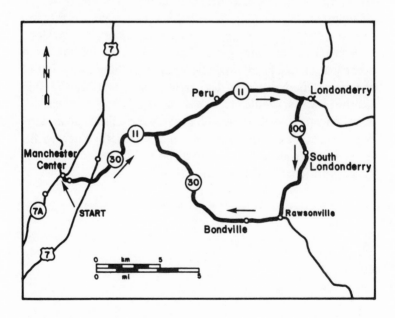

and uphill past Bromley Ski area through swamps and forests to its junction with Route 100 in Londonderry. Turn right, following 100 through South Londonderry to Rawsonville. Here you meet Route 30 once more. Follow this latter route west (right) through quiet woodlands to its intersection with Route 11.

Now, as you retrace your steps back past the Ranger Station and downhill to Manchester, you'll get glimpses of the wide valley, Mt. Equinox and other peaks, plus the hills of New York State beyond and to your west.

And I repeat: almost anywhere you go in Vermont, the trip is worth the effort. There are scores of state and municipal parks and forests. A study of the latest Vermont Official State Map (free at information centers or by request from the Agency of Transportation or the Agency of Development and Community Affairs, both in Montpelier) will show the location of dozens of them.

Remember: when you are in the woods you may not be alone —especially in hunting season. There's a reason for hunters to wear that highly visible red and orange clothing in the fall of the year. One November day, right in deer and bear hunting season, I was scheduled to take some Middlebury College students on a tree identification hike. We were a little late in starting, however, as I had to send one student back for a new outfit. She had showed up for the woodland walk dressed in a nice, furry, full-length racoon coat.

90

4

Patchwork Quilt

BACK TO NATURE

A century and more ago Vermont's landscape was 75 percent open and only 25 percent wooded. Now the figures are reversed. The interspersion of woods and open fields lends a patchwork quilt aspect to the scenery, giving much of the state its charm.

But, as I've already pointed out, fields do not stay fields without lots of help. They soon revert to forest. It's the process, from open land to woodland, that leads to a fascinating variety in the plants and animals of such an area. They come on stage awhile, then give way to others like performers in an all-star revue.

Thus in our 25 percent of open land you may see almost any of Vermont's trees or shrubs or wildlife. Two friends of mine saw a bobcat perched on a telephone pole, for instance, within a baseball's throw of the Starksboro School. It had probably wandered there from the woods beyond the schoolyard. And right in the middle of a field near Salisbury I watched a coyote pouncing and jumping for grasshoppers, apparently heedless of the traffic a few hundred yards away.

As the open land begins to close, so to speak, grass gives way to shrubs and flowers. These produce a tangle that makes wonderful living quarters for animals. One study showed more than a hundred meadow voles (meadow mice) per acre. These brownish four-inch rodents with the abbreviated tail and almost-hidden ears help themselves to a variety of greenery: stems, leaves, flowers, grass, and roots.

The whitetail deer may find an overgrown field to be one large "edge" as the forest creeps in from the sides. The buds and twigs of shrubs and seedlings are right where it can reach them, acre after acre. Woodcutters often find deer coming to visit where they've been working deep in the forest. The tops of trees and brush from a logging operation make unexpected and wonderful browse.

With such a brushland bonanza on every hand, the deer have made a marvelous comeback from a low point toward the end of the last century. At that time the whitetail deer was almost wiped out north of Rutland. A few dozen specimens were actually released and anxiously watched in an effort to restore their numbers. Now, just in annual hunting and roadside kills alone, deer are counted in the tens of thousands.

The little cottontail rabbit finds such brushland to its liking if it is somewhat open. Wild blackberry and raspberry create a pocket-sized jungle (remember Br'er Rabbit and his briar patch?) allowing both basic needs of wildlife to be satisfied at once: food and shelter.

COTTONTAIL RABBIT

The first plant colonizers of the fields are tough little pioneers. There's meadowsweet or hardhack bush, for instance, with its wiry brownish stems and small fragrant white blossoms. Its cousin, the steeplebush, has woolly leaves and a spire of pinkish blooms. Seeds of forest trees drift over the area and take root, among them the feathery parachutes of willow and poplar and the winged samaras of ash and maple.

One of our most stately open-grown trees often gets its start in a field or fencerow: the American elm. Its small disklike samaras flutter away on summer winds like confetti. Elm grows gracefully from a central trunk, arching like a

AMERICAN ELM

huge vase of flowers. Its double-toothed leaves feel as rough on top as on the underside. I once taught a natural history course to a group from the New York Institute for the Blind; they called elm the "sandpaper tree" from the scratchy surface of its leaves.

Tough and nearly unsplittable, elm wood was used as hubs for covered wagons on the rough road west. Dutch elm disease, an unauthorized European alien, has ruined millions of trees and robbed thousands of American streets of their shade. Now, as a result, the elm is pathetically easy to identify: it's that pale gaunt skeleton of pasture and roadside.

A much smaller tree, the alder, has male blossoms that look somewhat like stretched-out pussywillows. The female catkins develop dry little seeds that are sought by many birds. In the process, enough seeds are scattered on the wind so "there's always alders to cut," as a farmer told me when I asked what he did in his spare time.

This oversized shrub—or maybe it's an undersized tree—produces several trunks from a single base, as if from an underground flowerpot. Its smooth dark gray-green bark is punctuated by many raised dots, or lenticels.

Alder often grows with wet feet, so its presence may indicate underground water. This would be a happy circumstance in our arid southwest but a possible embarrassment of riches in already-moist Vermont. So if you're thinking of buying a plot of land on which alders are growing, don't ignore them. And don't say I didn't tell you.

Somewhat drier soil is preferred by the gray birch. With its triangular leaves, white bark, and three-cornered black blotches where trunk and branch meet, it's among the first trees in an overgrown field. It's often joined by its neighbor, the trembling aspen, or popple, with light gray-green bark and rounded fluttering leaves.

These first trees, growing quickly and dying in a few years, have an important role to play. Sometimes known as "nurse

GRAY BIRCH

trees'' by foresters, they serve as shelter for the species that will come later. Sugar maple, with its tasty buds and twigs, may thus escape the attention of deer and rodents as it comes up through a thicket of alders, or of its prolific cousin, the red maple. Tolerant of shade, the sugar maple struggles into the sunshine and eventually takes over from its neighbors.

There's a bit of living history along the edge of a field. Back when the area was cleared, birds sat on the fences or used them as flyways from one field to another. Foxes and rodents traveled these avenues as well. Stopping to rest or relieve itself, a bird or mammal may deposit the undigested remains of its last meal—the pits of chokecherry, for instance, or the seeds of sumac—in its droppings. Left there, complete with a little pat of fertilizer, a seed may germinate and thus speed the process of land reclamation. Burdock plants spring up where some creature pulled the scratchy stickers from its pelt. Grape and bittersweet and poison ivy (which doesn't seem to bother most animals—just people) record the visit of some bird or mammal.

Many a creature thus leaves its traces. Squirrels hide nuts and acorns. Foxes deposit berry seeds along with rodent bones and other undigestibles. The raccoon—always ready to try anything—may be responsible for all sorts of greenery. In this way the edge of a field or an overgrown fencerow becomes a wildlife bulletin board.

Such an area, rich in edibles, affords a good living for that portly ground-dwelling squirrel, the woodchuck. An inveterate burrower, the ten-pound rodent creates a maze of tunnels with several entrances. Most of the woodchuck's neighbors know of these holes and may use them in case of emergency. After a brush fire more than twenty refugees were found in one set of woodchuck tunnels.

Not all the woodchuck's neighbors regard it with unbridled enthusiasm, however. Johnny Chuck, as Thornton Burgess called him, has incurred the ire of many a gardener as he samples beans and melons and spinach with maddening equanimity. Nor does it help much to point out that the woodchuck was here first—*we* are the intruders, rather than the other way around.

Luckily, the news is not all bad. After a nonstop lunch in late summer, the waddling rodent hies itself off to a cozy den below the ground. There it will sleep until, according to legend, it will be the eagerly awaited star of Groundhog Day.

The 'chuck feeds mainly on tender items like clover and dandelions. It pays scant attention to plants that make tougher chewing: woody shrubs like the red osier dogwood with its scarlet branches, for instance, and the bushy panicled dogwood with

WOODCHUCK

abundant white autumn berries. Both these opposite-branched shrubs are common along fences and roadsides. There they may congregate as scraggly free-form native hedges.

You may also see Virginia creeper or five-leaved ivy climbing over walls and extinct trees. It clings tightly by means of tendrils that end in adhesive disks, giving rise to another name, woodbine. It's also called "scarlet ivy" for its brilliant color in the fall.

Woodbine's first cousin, the wild grape, also drapes itself from one tree to the next. Its sour little fruit clusters are sweetened by a good freeze, leading to the name of frost grape. It was the puckery taste of the unfrozen fruit, high out of reach, that led the impatient fox in the fable to declare them inedible anyway—sour grapes.

Down below those vines and shrubs you may find the common brake, or bracken fern. Its horizontal leaves, each with many leaflets, are borne in threes, atop a single stalk. In some sunny areas the bracken forms of a solid knee-high stand of green.

A close relative, the sensitive fern, has large and coarse leaves that seem to belie its name. With the first frost, however, it quickly dies. Then only the erect, spore-bearing stalks are left, like upright strings of brown beads. These give rise to another name, bead fern.

BRACKEN FERN

SENSITIVE FERN

Wild rose can be found in those overgrown fields; so can raspberry and blackberry, plus their trailing cousin, the dewberry, with sweet fruit close to the ground. Several kinds of wild mustard may blanket a whole field with their cross-shaped yellow flowers.

Also yellow is the cinquefoil, with five-petaled flowers plus leaves made of five leaflets each. We used to call this clover-sized plant the five-finger. Its white-flowered relative, the wild strawberry, makes wonderful jams and jelly—if you're patient enough to get more than a handful of the tiny fruit.

There's black-eyed susan with showy yellow petals and a convex brown central disc, plus its look-alike cousins—all often called coneflowers. Asters by the dozen in colors ranging from white to deep purple put on a showing in late summer, as do an equal number of goldenrods.

Coneflowers, asters, and goldenrods belong in the daisy family. So does that European import, the aromatic-leaved milfoil, or yarrow, with fernlike foliage and tiny white (rarely pink) blooms. On summer walks with youngsters at camp I often tell my small companions that yarrow has been used as a dried powder to stop nosebleed. Then, after I have them take a whiff of that woodsy-smelling foliage, I suggest they send a sprig home in a letter. Counselors tell me of campers dutifully sending a letter home—complete with yarrow leaves. Quite likely this is the only correspondence many a parent receives from camp all season.

Resembling yarrow, but with an umbrella-topped mass of minute white blossoms, is wild carrot or Queen Anne's lace. You may recall meeting this plant along the roadside in Chapter 2. It's also called birdsnest from the appearance of the dried fruiting clusters as they curl upwards and stand on their sturdy stalks all winter.

The central cones of coneflowers stay on their stems as well. So do the pods of milkweed—letting go a few of their fluffy parachute-seeds with each storm. Dropping to earth somewhere, they'll develop into those husky green plants with opposite leaves, fragrant pink flower clusters, and the sticky milky sap that was once used as a rather sorry substitute for rubber during the Second World War.

Projecting well above the snow, the winter fruits of summer plants are a valuable source of food for many of our birds. The fuzzy red clusters of staghorn sumac, for instance, are often visited by woodpeckers and chickadees—but not for the seeds. The birds are after insects and spiders that have taken refuge within the fruit mass. By spring the sumac bushes are pretty forlorn—bereft of almost every seed.

Staghorn sumac, by the way, is a much more friendly plant than the notorious poison sumac. Both have pinnately compound leaves of seven or more leaflets, but the fruit of poison sumac

STAGHORN SUMAC

hangs down, like a loose bunch of tiny waxy-white grapes. Besides, poison sumac grows in wet places, while the staghorn species prefers dry hillsides and fencerows.

Incidentally, poison oak and poison ivy are also in the sumac family. They, too, have white berries. Their compound leaves have just three leaflets ("leaves three—let it be").

Ambling along among all this herbage and shrubbery is a creature, once rare, that's extending its range every year, the Virginia opossum. Gifted with an anything-goes digestion, this New World relative of the kangaroo has apparently been aided in its northward junket by a proliferation of bird feeders, small gardens, and the inviting avenues of superhighways reaching north from more temperate climes.

The meandering marsupial's explorations are not without their price, however. One wintry day a friend brought me a 'possum he had found just south of Burlington. The last third of that long, almost hairless, prehensile tail was stiff and frozen. The thin ears were half gone from frostbite. It was a sorry sight, indeed.

I was headed south for Connecticut a day later, so I took the forlorn creature down with me to a garbage dump used by several summer camps in season. Since the opposum can climb and snoop into everything, its introduction may have been

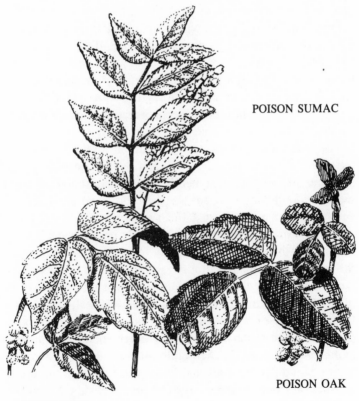

POISON SUMAC

POISON OAK

POISON IVY

attended with mixed emotions the next summer. I don't know—
I've never gone back to ask.

Down among the grassroots you may find a few of Vermont's native reptiles. There's the common garter snake, for instance, with three longitudinal stripes on a black background. It feeds on frogs, earthworms, and—on one occasion at least that I witnessed—the young of ground-nesting birds.

There's also the shy little green snake, perfectly colored to match its grassy surroundings. More rocky regions may shelter the black rat snake, with uniformly black back, white throat, and an underside that's white with dark blotches.

Sometimes the rat snake will vibrate its tail when disturbed. So will the milk snake, or checkered adder. If the tail happens to be in dry leaves or grass the resulting buzz may sound like a rattlesnake. Even if it just lies there without moving, the milk snake's coppery brown color alternating with lighter blotches on head and body will make it a copperhead for sure—and every summer I get the telephone calls to prove it.

The milk snake probably got its name from the habit of entering barns in search of mice. The startled farmer, seeing such a creature, apparently assumed it was there to steal milk from the cows—although how any sensitive bossy would stand for such treatment is more than I can imagine.

All these snakes are harmless—although, understandably, they may defend themselves if threatened. Our only poisonous snake, the rare and endangered timber rattler, has two heat-sensitive facial pits, larger than nostrils, that help it locate its warm-blooded prey. In addition, its eyes have a vertical, slitted, cat-like pupil. The eyes of our harmless local snakes have a round pupil. "So if you're in doubt about whether a northeastern snake is poisonous or not," a herpetologist once told his students, "get down on your hands and knees and look it in the eye."

Frogs and toads of the overgrown field include the common

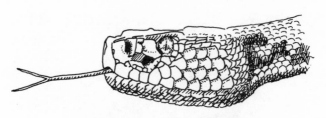

POISONOUS TIMBER RATTLER

NON-POISONOUS GRASS SNAKE

grass frog, or leopard frog. Green or brown with dark oval spots, it's often found far from water—even in the woods. The eastern tree frog, colored gray like the bark, may sing its loud staccato trill in May and June from halfway up a tree.

A spring peeper may join the tree frog in bush or tree; the sticky round pads on the toes of both allow them to cling wherever they land. I once saw a tree frog launch out after a moth, snap it up in mid-air, and land safely with a solid *plop* on another limb six feet away—and the whole performance taking place twenty feet above the earth.

The American toad bumps its warty way over the ground and through the grass mostly at night. One used to sit beneath the window of my study and snap up the insects that tumbled to the earth after they'd careened into my lighted window. And in case you wonder if you can get warts from a toad, the answer is an unqualified *yes*—if you're a baby toad. Otherwise, no.

Young frogs and toads, as is well known, get their start in the spring. Often the parents lay those jellylike eggs in small

AMERICAN TOAD

pools that will be dry in just a few weeks. This seems a short-sighted way to do things. Why not deposit the eggs in ponds that will remain all summer?

There is a logical, practical answer. Those part-time "vernal pools," as they are called, are usually without any predators. Hence the tadpoles have a better chance to survive. If the pond starts to dry rapidly, the tadpoles have an answer for that, too. They speed up the production of legs, develop lungs to replace the gills, and hastily leave their failing mudhole.

You'll find red eft salamanders in brushlands just as you did in the woods. The little creatures seem to be everywhere. After years on the land they head (1) downhill and (2) toward the largest open patch of sky—two acts that may lead them to a stream or pond. There they'll grow upper and lower fins on the tail. They'll change to olive-brown above and yellow beneath, and be back in the watery element they left as salamander teenagers so long ago.

THE BIRDS AND BEES

As for the bird life of these overgrown fields, some people can take them while others leave them. My wife finds it difficult to realize that her enthusiasm for birds is not shared by everybody. To her—and to several million others in the United States—these colorful creatures are fascinating indeed. An estimated fifty percent of our population takes some interest in birds.

The other fifty percent, however, doesn't give a hoot. Caring nothing for Life Lists and Christmas Bird Counts, they wouldn't know a Great Crested Grab from a No Left Tern. At times I wish this latter group were larger—especially as I watch while some avid birder, maneuvering for a glimpse of a feathered friend in a tree, tramples down a bed of violets.

Violets or not, a field on its way back to being a forest may be a home for almost anything in feathers. A single dead tree can be a veritable avian zoo.

There's the yellow-shafted flicker, for instance. Brown-speckled, with a red patch on the back of its head and a black band across the chest, the bird may hollow out a cavity near the top of a stub for its nest. Such tactics give this large woodpecker another name, high-hole.

That hole may be occupied for years, and not just by flickers. The robin-sized sparrow hawk, or kestrel, often uses such cavities to raise its young. You can spot a kestrel by its size (small for a hawk), black and white facial pattern, red tail, and pointed wings when flying. Sometimes it teeters when sitting on a wire or tall perch, as if unsure of its balance.

That blatant, pushy bird, the starling, may move right into a tree cavity that's still occupied by another bird. Its speckled dark plumage with metallic sheen is easy to recognize, as is its yellow bill, especially in spring. Sometimes a flock of starlings will land at one end of a field, spread out, and walk right down the field in a skirmish line. Busily flicking leaves and dead grass, these European upstarts may atone for their brazen

YELLOW-SHAFTED FLICKER

ways a bit as they snap up hundreds of insects along the way.

The gentle bluebird may nest in that hole, as will the graceful tree swallow. The two look somewhat alike, but the bluebird's back is sky blue, while that of the tree swallow is iridescent, sometimes almost green. The bluebird's rusty-red breast contrasts with the swallow's white underside, as well.

Swallows catch their food on the wing. The bluebird has the characteristic habit of sitting on a low wire or shrub, dropping down for a bit of food, and flying back again to almost the same spot.

That same cavity may be occupied another time by a family of chickadees, or even by a house wren—although this tiny brown chatterbox usually prefers a lower situation. One pair of wrens raised a brood in the pocket of an old jacket hanging inside a shed door.

The red-tailed hawk will use that high stub for a lookout. Robins and redwinged blackbirds often proclaim their territory from on high. So does the long-tailed brown thrasher and its gray and white cousin, the mockingbird. Another cousin, the almost all-gray catbird, prefers the lower bushes.

Looking somewhat like the mockingbird is the northern shrike, with gray body, black mask and wings, and heavy black beak. The shrike flies low to the ground and then rises suddenly to

RED-TAILED HAWK

109

a high perch. There it remains, looking for bird or mouse or insect. When it catches its prey the shrike may impale it for later use on a thorn or barbed wire. Hence it is also known as the butcherbird. You can tell when there's a shrike around: all the other birds will "freeze" until danger is past. Even the boisterous blue jay is silent and watchful when the smaller bird is near.

A flock of crows may leave one of their number as a sentinel on that high tree while they go about their search for new-planted corn or insects or anything that might pass as food. When a crow lands in an area and the small birds seem agitated, the crow will continue walking this way and that. By the intensity of their cries, the victims may actually lead the crow to their nest.

This doesn't work with all birds, however. The redwinged blackbird is quick to fly to the attack. It may be joined by others of its kind, plus the gravel-voiced, long-tailed common grackle —itself no saint around other birds' nests. The crow flees in haste, trailing an outraged retinue of redwings and grackles until they've routed their enemy. Then they return in triumph.

Nor does the crow stay long in kingbird territory. The slate gray kingbird with white belly and white band on the tip of its tail is well named: it is monarch of its own domain. A kingbird will "ride" a crow or hawk until the larger bird is vanquished— often minus several feathers.

One lady, new to the ways of birds, described the antics of a flock of blackbirds after a crow. "When it dived, they would dive," she said. "When it turned right or left they would follow. It was so charming to see a mother bird training her babies to fly like that."

These past years there's been another presence in the skies, the turkey vulture. This large scavenger has worked its way north from the mid-Atlantic states along with the mockingbird, cardinal, and the little gray tufted titmouse. These birds scarcely showed up on Vermont bird counts a generation ago except as curiosities. Now they are fairly common and the leisurely flight of the "T.V.," as birders call the vulture, can be seen clear into Canada north of Montreal.

You can tell the T.V. from almost any other large soaring bird because the vulture holds its wings just a bit above the horizontal, in a very shallow letter "V." It tips and tilts as if the wind currents were almost upsetting it, but that's merely a manner of flight. In reality that naked red head—so ugly to our eyes but so perfectly adapted to digging into decaying flesh without getting feathers mussed—is turning this way and that to keep an incredibly keen eye out for its next meal.

The bushes and scattered trees will reveal the familiar blue jay, with jaunty crest, black chin strap, and blue and white plumage. About the same size is the mourning dove. The dove's smallish head and white-sided pointed tail help identify it on a limb or telephone wire even if you cannot see the iridescence on its brownish feathers.

BLUE JAY

On the ground beneath is the ground robin or chestnut-sided towhee, so named for its robin-red sides. Its upper portions are black while the breast is white. The towhee sounds like half a dozen birds as it furiously scratches for food, making the dry leaves fly so the bird itself may be hidden. More common in southern parts of the state, it's sometimes called chewink after the sound of its call note. The full song—a lilting, emphatic "drink your teeeeee"—can be heard in brushland all the way to Florida.

These days a field may contain a ringnecked pheasant or two; the colorful, longtailed game birds have been released in many parts of Vermont. The pheasant is an Asiatic species while its large relative, the wild turkey, is distinctly American. You may see the turkey in fields and cultivated areas, especially if grain has been harvested there recently.

The effervescent tinkling of the bobolink, with a song sounding like its name, may lead you to a glimpse of the bird. Singing on rapidly beating wings that point downward in flight, it is sometimes called "skunkbird"—not because of any bodily perfume but because it is black below and mostly white above.

Like its bobolink cousin, the common meadowlark nests in the grass. It sometimes comes to grief with our modern methods of getting two or three hay crops per season. The nests are often destroyed with the first cut. Nevertheless, the brownish meadowlark with white-sided tail and a black "V" crossing its yellow breast still sings its high, clear whistle from tree stub or utility pole. Then it soars out over the meadow on rapidly beating wings, followed by a glide and a sudden drop into the grass.

One of the meadowlark's most colorful relatives is the northern oriole. Striking in orange and black, it's almost the size of a robin. Its deep hanging nest, woven of grasses and string, must give the youngsters a wild ride as it tosses at the end of its slender branch in a summer storm. You often see oriole nests toward the tips of bare limbs, especially elms, after the leaves have fallen.

NORTHERN ORIOLE

A friend of mine, Lillian Birkett, puts out different colored yarn for the orioles each year. She has been able to collect several of the resulting works of art: yellow nests, blue nests, and a holiday-colored red and green nest she hangs in her Christmas tree.

Even if there was room to name them all, the roster of birds would never be complete. The changing scene among the vegetation would see to that. The oriole would leave as other trees filled in, but its half-size look-alike, the redstart (actually a black and orange warbler) would find itself right at home. Those wild canaries, the goldfinches, would seek more open land, as would the brown-streaked song sparrow. They'd be replaced by thrushes and other woodland birds.

113

A farmer plowing a field is sometimes attended by hundreds of ringbilled gulls. These birds follow the plow to pick earthworms and grubs from the soil. Later in the same field, especially when manure is spread in winter, you may see flocks of horned larks. Brown above and whitish beneath, the larks have a black patch beneath a white or yellow throat. They wheel above a field, drop to earth—and seem to disappear, so closely do they match their surroundings. The twin points of feathers, or "horns," at the rear of the head may not be visible.

Almost any gravelly land may serve as a nesting place for the killdeer. This robin-sized bird runs over the ground on its long legs, or cries out its name as it flies. It is brown above and white below with two black bands across the breast.

The killdeer lays its eggs right on the ground; the young can run from the nest shortly after they're hatched. A killdeer made

RINGBILLED GULL

KILLDEER

her home at the far edge of the sandy outfield on the baseball diamond in my town of Lincoln. We drew a circle around the nest, and anybody who hit a ball within that circle was automatically out.

Birds give the hordes of insects more attention than their leggy victims might wish. Flycatchers of several sizes dart out from a chosen limb after a hapless beetle or mosquito. Sometimes you can hear the snap of the bird's beak a hundred feet away.

Warblers search every inch of tree and shrub. Woodpeckers hammer away after grubs and borers, and the flicker settles down near an anthill for a peppery meal. Even the cedar waxwing in natty olive uniform, black mask, and little waxy tips to the wing feathers may forsake a diet of blueberries and cedar fruit to snatch a passing fly. Once I watched half a dozen cedar waxwings in an early snowstorm, darting out optimistically after the big drifting flakes.

Where the birds leave off, so to speak, some kinds of insects may take over. Dragonflies course back and forth over meadow and pasture and brushland, scanning the air with those great compound eyes. Bristly legs held in basket fashion, the dragonflies scoop gnats and mosquitoes in mid-flight. Then they eat them as they go, like a strolling youngster with an ice cream cone.

Scanning the earth at your feet you may discover dark-colored ground beetles, seeking almost anything that moves. Brightly colored tiger beetles half run, half fly across an open area or exposed ledge—fully as ferocious as their tropical namesakes. Even the gentle-appearing ladybird beetle, or ladybug, slices its way through a massed colony of aphids like an animated mowing machine.

Then there's the praying mantis, with its viselike forelegs cocked to lash out at an insect meal. Its pixie face bears two great compound eyes and tiny pointed chin and looks strangely human as it turns its head and soberly surveys you. This green-brown immigrant from the south may be as much as four inches long. It stands high on four of its legs—the front two held as in prayer, ready to seize a victim. A friend of mine, observing the pious attitude that preceded the grisly meal, decided the mantis was saying grace.

Wasps take a different approach to their prey. Some carnivorous types lay eggs that hatch into hungry little grubs on their caterpillar hosts. Others drag the caterpillars off to be consumed elsewhere.

Whitefaced hornets, whose newly abandoned paper nests you discover after the leaves have fallen, seek flies to carry back to their young. Indeed, one hornet, called the horse guard, patrols the flanks of its equine companion for just such a purpose.

Among the spider population one of the most impressive nets is spread by the large northern garden spider. Yellow and black and white, the spider waits in the center of a strong elastic web—circular strands, radiating supports, and all. There's usually a thick zigzag ribbon of white silk at the center, a warning, possibly, for creatures too large to be edible. From

116

PRAYING MANTIS

this may come the farmhouse custom of putting a wisp of white cotton on a door screen to repel flies.

Other spiders—weavers, funnel-web builders, wolf spiders —make their homes in the meadow. Their cousins, the harvestmen or daddy longlegs, capture tiny insects and mites, even as other mites cling to the harvestmen like fleas on a dog.

One disconcerting development in our Green Mountain State and much of our northeast is the uninvited presence of a pushy little intruder from the Old World: the European earwig. The entomology book I studied in college lists it as ''rare''—which may show how long ago I went to school. Now the persistent little insect, half an inch long and with a pair of pinchers adorning its rear, has snooped and sneaked into almost any crevice that'll shelter its shiny brown body. You'll find it under bits

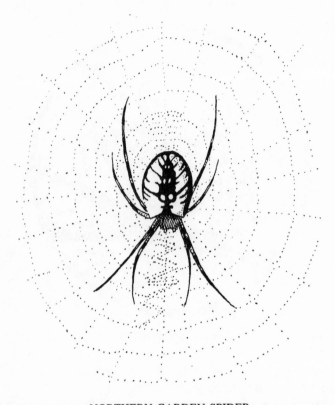

NORTHERN GARDEN SPIDER

of loose bark, house shingles, even under the pail or box you set down a few hours ago.

This is how it behaves during the day. At night the earwig sallies forth on its own version of high adventure. And ''high'' is often the case: the intrepid little insect trots up tree trunks, rambles over rocks, and saunters along scaffolding seeking anything edible—from the petals of your choicest garden flowers to the crumbs from a weekend picnic.

And how does one deal with these blatent little busybodies? Sprinkles of pepper across the threshold of doors have helped;

so have the biologically acceptable toxins rotenone and pyrethrum, derived from plants the creatures don't like. And when I checked the official pronouncement from our local county authorities I learned it was "good not to leave anything undisturbed for any length of time"—which brought up interesting mental pictures of a household busily shifting tables and chairs on Tuesdays and Thursdays, with books and sofas on Monday, Wednesday, and Friday.

With the exception of the birds and a cricket or two, much of this teeming life carries on in silence. At least it is silent to our ears—and at least until mid-summer. Then begins the season of insect sound.

It seems the most musical of the common insects are the winged adults of the grasshopper family. The field cricket lived through the winter and already has its wings but most of its jumping relatives began the new year not as recognizable insects but as eggs. Hatching in the spring, those eggs produced tiny active nymphs. The nymphs possessed mere buds where wings would grow. Shedding their outer skin several times these youngsters became more like their parents with each moult. Now, at least, they have become adults—wings and all. And it's the wings that allow them to sing.

Some hoppers rub one wing against the other, like crickets.

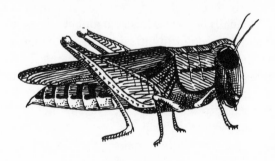

GRASSHOPPER

Others scratch the wings against the body or snap them in flight with a crackling sound. Still others rub leg against wing, using those powerful hind legs, which are provided with scrapers for the purpose.

Once I found a grasshopper that had lost both hind legs so it could not spring into the air. It was a species that crackles its wings in flight, so I tossed it aloft. Away it went, over grassland and bushes, in what I assume was a paroxysm of gratitude —crackling all the way.

It's almost entirely the males that are so gifted. The females, apparently attracted by the sound, join them for mating. Some males, like the snowy tree cricket, may sing in concert—each joining the others in perfect rhythm.

The activities of the tree cricket, as with other insects, are influenced by the temperature. The warmer it is, the faster they move. The same is true of insect song. Indeed, if you can time the musical trill of the snowy tree cricket, you'll have a pretty good idea of the temperature. Count the number of trills in fifteen seconds. Add forty to this figure, and the resulting sum is the Fahrenheit temperature. A count of thirty trills plus forty would be seventy degrees, and so on. It's surprisingly accurate, too—unless the cricket's in the sun and everything else is in the shade.

There's also that shrill songster, the summer cicada, or "locust." Actually it's not a locust at all but a large cousin of the aphid and those colorful little denizens of the meadow, the leafhoppers. The cicada looks like a huge green fly with long membranous wings. It sings by vibrating special organs on its abdomen. Once our dog picked up what appeared to be a dead cicada. But when it burst to life the buzzing mouthful caused the pup to drop it with a yelp.

Then there are the colorful aerialists, the butterflies: the great black and yellow tiger swallowtail, for instance, plus the orange

MONARCH BUTTERFLY

and black monarch, and its smaller look-alike, the viceroy. Pale yellow cabbage butterflies dance over the grassland. Orange skippers bounce from one flower to another. White admirals, black swallowtails, silver-spangled fritillaries all began as stodgy caterpillars and changed into those dancing bits of color in one of the most dramatic transformations in nature.

A summer's night may be filled with fireflies, or lightning bugs. These soft-winged beetles cruise the air above the meadow. Their mates, known as glowworms, creep through the grass. Even the eggs laid by many glowworms are luminescent, as are the larvae themselves.

Day and night it continues, aboveground and below. At dusk the bats leave their caves and attics and hollow trees to take up where the birds and wasps and dragonflies left off. Beneath the soil the mole plows along with its spadelike forefeet, seeking grubs and worms. Those many-legged crustaceans, the sow bugs, leave the shelter of their flat rock or grass clump. Away they go, foraging for bits of plant and animal material. They're not above finishing off a wounded insect if they find one. These and many more are there—above and around and beneath you. All you have to do is look.

122

Where I'd Take You If I Could

Robert Frost Interpretive Trail. This enjoyable little walk covers scarcely a mile and can be done in less than an hour. The pathway is almost level and winds its way in a circle through forests, brush land, and pasture. It travels across a little bridge over a playful river and pays brief visits to this stream two more times along the way.

Maintained by the U.S. Forest Service, the trail begins at a parking lot across the road from the Robert Frost Wayside area. This area is on Vermont Route 125, about two miles east of Ripton. The trail has signposts every few hundred yards, each bearing selected writings of the late "poet laureate of Vermont." There are also a few benches at intervals, so the trail can be traveled by almost anybody.

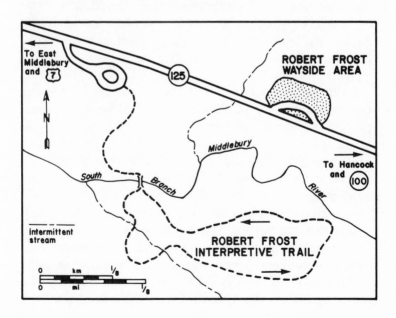

123

Although this is not a mountain path, the altitude is high enough to support the growth of the vegetation which occurs in less accessible areas. Labels help identify a number of the upland trees and many of the smaller plants you've met in these pages. Thus, you'll find yourself on intimate terms with balsam fir, alder, black cherry, sugar maple, blueberry, bracken fern, and a dozen of their green neighbors.

The trail area is open at any season. The pathway is not kept clear of snow, but it's a delight to travel if the drifts are not too deep. Cross country skiers often adapt a part of the pathway for their use. You may find the tracks of weasel, or fox, or snowshoe hare. I've seen signs of mink along the streambank, and there's a good chance of a deer in the meadows.

After your stroll you may wish to visit the Wayside Area across the road. Here you'll find rest rooms—not fancy, but adequate—and several picnic tables. It's a comfortable and popular little spot, about a mile west of the Bread Loaf campus of Middlebury College. It was at a summer school on this campus that I heard Ripton's famous resident recite his "Road Not Taken" early in my career as a writer.

Southern Vermont Loop. Uphill and down, border to border (and spanning two days if you wish), this 175-mile tour samples much of the southern third of Vermont. It takes you past farms going native after years of cultivation; alongside and across one of the northeast's major rivers; and over a state highway so steep it's provided with three escape ramps for runaway trucks.

At one point the trail passes the homes of more than a hundred active little summer visitors: bank swallows who travel half the globe to raise a family in Vermont. Along another road there's an excellent chance of spotting a wild turkey. Another route passes just a few miles from where an amorous bull moose cozied up for weeks to—of all things—a Vermont cow.

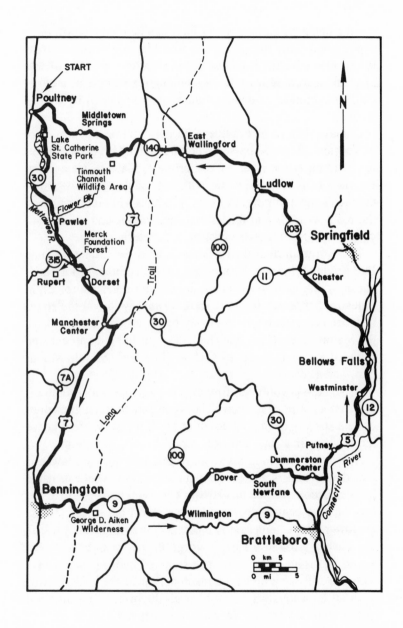

Let's begin with the turkeys. They can be found almost any-where—and especially along the first forty miles of our trip: Route 30 south from Poultney to Manchester. I've seen fifteen of them, searching for leftovers among the stubble of a corn-field. Sometimes, at dawn or dusk, they're joined by a deer or two.

Our tour begins at Poultney, on the extreme western edge of Vermont. Route 30 passes over the Poultney River as it leaves town. Look at the river as you cross it. Slabs of slate along the sides help keep the water within its banks. Slate is one of the area's most important natural products—in outcrops along the road, as walls and fences and foundations and, of course, as a sturdy roofing and construction material.

Three miles farther the road passes Lake St. Catherine State Park (right). This popular area has all the facilities—foot trails, nature trails, campsites, picnic areas, and much more. Eight miles farther (don't forget to look for turkeys along the edges of woods and fields) the highway bends around the rapids of the Mettawee River, on the right. To your left are half a dozen rounded knobs with names such as Bald Hill, Middle Moun-tain, and Haystack.

As you travel you'll see firewood stored up, even in summer, at farmhouses along the way. The wood may be in jumbled piles or neat stacks—even on a porch or in a garage, where it keeps the family car at bay until the wood is used next winter.

At Pawlet, fifteen miles south of Poultney, the Mettawee is joined by a creek whose boisterous waters seem to belie its name Flower Brook. To see this stream best, you must pause at the town's wide central crossroads. It's worth the stop.

Flower Brook, temporarily chastened by a little dam, escapes and dashes through a narrow gorge in the rocks beneath the Route 30 bridge. The dam once supplied hydro power there. You can still see a bit of the machinery near the bridge. Now some of its waters are piped beneath the bridge to a little red power station a few score yards downstream.

The brook races beneath Mach's General Store, there in the center of Pawlet. At the raised viewing platform in the rear of the store you can look straight down through the glass at the torrent fifty feet below. There you'll see the water-sculpted bedrock, the pebbly bottom, and perhaps a trout or two.

Southward once more on Route 30, follow the flat valley of the Mettawee. It's hard to realize this little river is responsible for the whole valley, but science says a river flows through a valley it has created.

The valley narrows as you go south. You're approaching the upper end of this northward-flowing river. You'll see little brooks tumbling down to it through mini-valleys of their own. Such a system (small streams flowing into a larger one, plus all the land thus drained) is called a watershed.

White birch clumps dot a pasture hillside about six miles south of Pawlet. The pasture is on the left, just before Route 315 goes right (west) to Rupert. The Merck Foundation near Rupert is one of my favorite natural areas, with forests and fields plus study and museum facilities. Much of the time it's necessary to walk a short distance to the center from a forested parking lot. I heartily recommend it as we continue south.

At the charming town of Dorset, turn to the right at the Dorset Inn off Route 30. Continue down grass-centered Church Street to its end at West Road. Go south (left) on West Road 1.8 miles. Turn up Nichols Hill Road (right) for a look in half a mile at one of the largest sugar maples in Vermont.

This gnarled old patriarch, on a lawn at the left side of the curving road, was slated for removal as a street improvement measure. The well-known artist W. Dean Fausett, who lived in the house at the time, had other wishes, however. After the resultant uproar the tree was saved. The tree stands there now. It is minus several limbs and is held together by a few long rods—but it's an impressive old timer nonetheless.

Backtrack to West Road and turn right. Soon you're on Route 30 again, headed south to Manchester Center, two miles away.

Cross Route 7A (a quick right, then left) and travel 1.5 miles to the new U.S. Route 7 south.

This route, opened in the early 1980s, affords a look at a recent roadway carved through a woodland. As you drive, note that the trees on either side are tall, slender, and almost unbranched. When the trees grow close together in a deep forest their lower limbs become shaded and drop away. This "self-pruning," as foresters call it, results in a woodland that looks almost like utility poles with leaves.

Notice the wind turbines high on the Equinox Ridge off to your right (west): there are several such modern windmills in Vermont. To your left you'll see little streams cascading to fill an occasional swamp or beaver pond.

Travel twenty miles of this highway and then take the exit leading to Route 9 toward Brattleboro (east). This road winds steeply uphill—indeed, it's so precipitous that there's a deep sand escape ramp for trucks whose brakes fail as they come down from the other direction.

About five miles from where you began on Route 9, the Long Trail crosses the road. Here it shares its pathway with the Appalachian Trail as both wend northward. Continue onward through rock cuts and mixed forests to a turnoff on the right. Peg and I have enjoyed a lunch beside the rushing stream here as we watched three ravens play overhead.

A sign announces the George D. Aiken Wilderness to your right (south) about five miles beyond that rest area. The hope is to preserve forever the natural countryside of which the long-time Senator from Vermont was so fond.

Continue east past beaver swamps and quiet forests. There's a brook along the road on the descent toward Wilmington. This is a portion of the watershed of the Deerfield River—itself a stream used repeatedly for hydroelectric power at little mills along its length.

Two more truck escape ramps to your right warn of the slope

of the hill down toward Wilmington. At this town turn left (north) on Route 100. This highway is well populated with shops and tourist attractions for four miles until the second turnoff to the right toward Dover. From Dover the road winds eastward, over hills, through mixed forests and quiet evergreens to South Newfane.

A mile beyond South Newfane the road goes through the 120-foot Williamsville covered bridge. A scarce two miles further, turn right (south) onto Route 30. Here you'll follow the West River briefly as it heads toward its junction with the Connecticut at Brattleboro.

After two miles along the West River take the Dummerston Center Road that turns left (east) through the Dummerston covered bridge. Its 280-foot length makes this bridge the longest in the state.

Now begins a twisting drive through Dummerston Center. If it happens to be the second Sunday in October you'll have plenty of company on the road. The area is famous for its autumn apple festival.

Two miles east of Dummerston Center the little road ends at U.S. Route 5. Turn left (north) toward Putney, which is about four miles up the road. You may be interested in Putney's wildflower nursery on the left. With hundreds of plants labeled it can be your private crash course in botany. There's also a little shop (Green Mountain Spinnery) in the town where the fleece of some of the countryside's four-footed residents is made into yarn.

Three miles beyond Putney, on the right, the rows of blueberry bushes tell of a relatively new enterprise in Vermont: pick-your-own-crops. Blueberries come along fairly late in summer; at other times and places you can harvest strawberries (June), raspberries (July), and apples (September). An eye to signs along the road may help you help yourself to a do-it-yourself harvest.

Along much of Route 5 you can view the broad Connecticut River. It begins in Quebec, forms the boundary between Vermont and New Hampshire, and makes its way through central Massachusetts and Connecticut to Long Island Sound.

The river valley provides admirable farming—on the Vermont side at least. A glance across it reveals that New Hampshire is not always so blessed. Many of the cliffs come down within a stone's throw of the water.

Continue north to the town of Westminster. Four miles beyond is the Bellows Falls High School (left). A bit further on the same side is a large sand bank. The many holes near its top, which have been there for years, are the summer homes of scores of bank swallows. These brown birds with white undersides crossed by a brown bib may come here from as far as Argentina. It's a mystery how these sociable little mosquito hawks with the buzzing call find their way.

And why do they come to this very sandbank year after year? I posed this question to a group of youngsters at the Bellows Falls grammar school and one girl had the answer. "I guess," she said, with obvious local pride, "it's because our mosquitoes must taste better."

Half a mile north of this sandbank you come to the first of two bridges that cross the river at Bellows Falls. Turning right over the first one (Route 12) just south of the town, you can look down upon the rugged rocks and the canal that bypasses the falls. There's also a concrete fish ladder to aid the river's finny denizens in their upstream run. In spawning season, visitors can watch the fish as they struggle against the current.

After crossing the Connecticut River, turn left (north) on Route 12 in New Hampshire. A mile farther north go left again back across the river to Vermont. There's more rocky streambed under the bridge, plus the narrow stretch of the canal. This first U.S. canal (1802) was created to provide shipping with a less exhilarating ride than bobbing along among those rocks.

Back at Route 5, turn north for three more miles. The backwaters of the river near the road are a favorite haunt of the great blue heron; we've seen four or five at once. Look for ducks as well, and an occasional swimming muskrat.

Bear left (west) onto Route 103. This road skirts rich farmlands along the Williams River. The yellow of poplars, the many-colored maples, and the scarlet woodbine and sumac make this a scenic drive in late September.

As you follow Route 103 through Chester, look for the town's famous stone houses along the highway. Shortly thereafter the road goes through steep-sided Proctorsville Gulf, whose rocky slopes are covered with vegetation—from tall trees to dark green Christmas ferns clinging to the scanty soil.

Peg and I have seen barred owls half hidden in the shadows of these trees. Gray-brown and streaked, a barred owl seems about the size of a chicken, sitting there in the gloom. If you notice a cluster of gray leaves in a sheltering tree, look again: the "leaves" may have feathers and large brown eyes.

The road continues through Ludlow, receiving Route 100 from the left and bidding it farewell to the right after 1.5 miles. Some ten miles later, turn left (west) off 103 onto Route 140 into East Wallingford.

About five miles north of this turnoff point, an oddball romance budded in a Shrewsbury pasture. For reasons of its own, a bull moose spent several autumn weeks in the company of Jessica, a farm heifer. Deserting its own kind, the great antlered beast sidled up to its domestic distant cousin.

The budding romance never blossomed. The attraction was apparently all one way. Shunning fame and fortune, Jessica never gave that moose a tumble.

Continue on Route 140 uphill and down, through forests, alongside extinct farms, and past idyllic open meadows. The road curves down through the woods, following the Roaring Brook ravine to U.S. Route 7 at Wallingford. Crossing Route 7 it continues its wandering ways.

Cattail swamps and beaver ponds greet you by the wayside

BARRED OWL

in the Tinmouth Channel Wildlife Management Area. Tall beeches, birches, and maples line the road beyond the swamp. Fields that are going back to forests bear diverse wild crops of burdock, highbush cranberry, and sumac.

The road makes its way through Middletown Springs past gnarled old sugar maples and more fields sneaking back to forests. East Poultney, with church and houses and village green, is a reminder of the many little towns you've seen along the way. Then, in scarcely two miles, the cross-the-state-twice circle is finished.

All told, the tour has spanned about 175 miles. Such a junket may be more than you'd care to tackle in a search for rustic Vermont with its fields that have gone back to nature. Actually, such fields aren't hard to find on almost any shorter trip. Not all all.

The woods are full of them.

5

Watery World

BROOKS AND BOGS AND BEAVER PONDS

It must be exhilarating to live in a stream. The water is forever on the move—grinding away at rocks here and cutting at a bank there. A sandbar in one spot today will be somewhere else tomorrow. A water dweller may have to keep moving just to stay in place.

The animals that call a stream their home are wonderfully tuned to their special way of life. Trout and dace are cylindrical in cross section to offer the least resistance to the current. Other fish burrow into the protective sand with just their eyes showing. Still others spend their entire lives in the shelter of a rock or log or possess fingerlike fins to help them cling to the bottom.

One beetle larva is so flat it looks like a little coin plastered against a rock. In fact it's called the water penny. Another beetle carries a bubble of air around with it—a self-contained Scuba outfit to allow it to breathe while submerged. There's even a beetle so completely at ease among sunken stems and pebbles that it cannot swim. If removed from its chosen spot it flounders helplessly in the water until it sinks back to safety.

The plants, too, must cope with this special world. Stream-side trees and bushes continually reach back to the shore with their roots as the water threatens to topple them. As a result the main trunk may be almost horizontal over the water while those supporting roots grope and sprawl inland.

Parts of underwater plants break off at special joints. These little adventurers get whisked away by the current to start a new life elsewhere. Mosses at the water's edge release tiny reproductive male cells into the layer of moisture that coats their surroundings. The cells swim in this thin film until they find a cooperative female cell, thus launching a new generation.

Look for liverworts along the streambank. They're flat, an inch or two in size and lobed, supposedly, like a tiny piece of green liver—hence the name. Their pebbly texture makes them look as if they've got goosebumps.

As you gaze at a liverwort, doff your hat. Ancestors of this nondescript little bit of life were among the first green plants to leave the water for the uncertainties of life on land. Apparently they never got very far; they're still clinging to places where it is moist.

LIVERWORT

Red maple, poplar, elm, and hemlock often strew their wind-born seeds on the waters, thus starting families downstream. Witch hazel, with its yellow wispy-petaled blossoms, produces seeds in little capsules. The capsules split with an audible snap, tossing the seeds as much as ten feet away. Those that land in the water may be borne for miles before they find hospitable lodging.

Streamside rocks and banks are often covered with a moisture loving fern, the common polypody. The brave little plant may grow where it's wildly tossed by clouds of mist, or even on a ledge directly behind the plunging sheet of a waterfall.

A much larger species, the ostrich fern, often grows in these damp situations. True to its name, the fern's leaves look like great ostrich plumes. Sometimes they are five feet long and a foot wide. They uncoil in typical fern fashion in spring. Their bottle-cap-size croziers provide thousands of gatherers with fiddleheads free for the picking—and more thousands of restaurant-goers with the same fiddleheads at fancy prices.

Fiddleheads are sought by deer, mice, squirrels, porcupines, and beavers. Indeed, many creatures join in the celebration of this gourmet meal. Some friends of mine drove to a wooded

OSTRICH FERN

swamp along the Black River near Ludlow, baskets in hand and ready for a morning's harvesting. "But we came in last," Bea Hallock said ruefully. "Half the wildlife in Windsor County beat us to it. Tracks all over the place, and not enough fiddleheads for a tossed salad."

Another swampland crop that Peg and I enjoy is the cowslip, or marsh marigold. You can find it along almost any streamside in early May. Its thick, rounded leaves appear soon after the frost has left the ground for good.

Borne on short fleshy stalks, the leaves make wonderful spring greens. Brought to a boil in two changes of water to temper their spring tonic taste, marsh marigolds are a welcome relief from the tired old grocery fare. We usually cook and freeze several containers of them: they sure can start you wishing on a cold winter day.

Often cowslips almost hide the remains of last year's grasses in a wet meadow, so densely do they grow. Their bright yellow flowers look like buttercups—and, indeed, they are of the same family as that common pasture plant. We like them best just when they are in bud.

Streamsides in the southern half of our state may play host to that smelly harbinger of spring, the skunk cabbage. Recognized by the pointed green and purple hood sheltering its yellow flower spike, the skunk cabbage has been called "the plant that builds its own greenhouse."

It seems that in late winter the dormant bud, well below the ground, speeds up its metabolic processes. This results in the production of excess heat, softening the frozen soil and allowing the musky plant to get a headstart on the season. Later the broad leaves, fully as large as those of its garden namesake, generously bestow their aroma on your boots and surrounding area when you step on them.

Skunk cabbage is sometimes confused with the more abundant large-leaved plant, the false hellebore. The large-plaited leaves of the latter look as if they've been folded along the

SKUNK CABBAGE

prominent ribs. The yellow-green flowers are borne in a large cluster. Look at a flower closely and you'll be reminded of the familiar Easter lily. Sure enough, Indian poke, as it's also called, is a relative of the lily—and of onion and garlic, for that matter. But don't try it—it's a potent poison.

The fetid odor of skunk cabbage calls carrion flies and sexton beetles, which explore the hooded blossoms and thereby pollinate the plant. Sometimes the northern yellow-throated warbler makes its nest among those pungent leaves—and, I suppose, from the skunk cabbage's point of view, there goes the neighborhood.

The eastern phoebe nests along these streams, as well. It often chooses the underside of a bridge or the shelter of a convenient ledge. You can recognize this gray-brown flycatcher with whitish underside by the way it repeatedly bobs its tail. Often, as it flies out to snatch a passing insect, you can hear its beak snap—sometimes even before you've noticed the bird.

Along a wooded shore you may discover a solitary sandpiper. Somewhat smaller than a robin, this longlegged shorebird nods constantly as it searches for worms and insects. It's a cousin to that feathered oddball, the woodcock.

Eyes located high on its head give the chunky brown woodcock a ridiculous look. It walks with a slow, mincing step—then stops and probes in the damp soil with its flexible bill, feeling for earthworms. A voice like a tinny Bronx cheer is in startling contrast to an ecstatic chirping made by its wings in courtship flight high above the earth. Small wonder it labors under a variety of names: bog sucker, swamp chicken, night partridge, bigeyes, and timber doodle.

Perched in a tree above a pool may be a belted kingfisher—named for its blue-gray breast band and its habit of plunging into the water after a finny dinner. Somewhat larger than a robin, the bird has a disreputable crest of tousled-looking feathers plus a staccato call that sounds more like a baby's rattle than a bird.

Among the mammals of the streams, the otter and mink may travel into the smallest brook in their search for fish, crayfish, and frogs. You might glimpse the twenty-pound otter along many rivers—including Otter Creek, which is Vermont's most extensive river system. Look for summer mud ramps and winter snowslides made by this rollicking creature as it climbs up a bank and careens down into the stream. It reminds you of a kid at a commercial water slide—except the otter gets its ride for free.

The one-pound mink is less playful but just as active. It prowls large rivers, lakes, and little woodland streams. Sometimes it travels overland. Once my father and I watched as a mink stealthily filched every worm from the bait box of a fisherman snoozing over his pole on the bank of Lake Dunmore.

One of the commonest tracks in the mud along a stream is the handlike print of the raccoon. Probing industriously through the sand and mud with those sensitive paws, it sozzles almost

OTTER

everything in the water as if washing it before eating. It will wash a frog, a salamander, a beetle. It will even wash a fish.

If you're lucky you may spot the water shrew. It's larger than its tiny cousins with, I suppose, a proportionately larger appetite. It can dive and swim and even hunt its food under the ice. The first water shrew I ever saw was the most memorable: it actually ran across the water. Large hairs on its big hind feet plus a water-repellent coat allow this mouse-sized creature to scamper across a pool without breaking through the surface film.

The shrew's achievement would be a ho-hum performance for one of the most familiar of aquatic insects: the water strider. You'll see it on almost any pool. Spreading its weight on long toes, this slender black bug spends its life skating across the surface. Its keen eyes note everything that falls to the water, and it will even jump into the air after a gnat or mosquito. The dimples made in the surface film by the strider's feet cause bright circles of sunlight on the bottom. When agitated, a group of water striders will dash about so the individual insects disappear in the confusion of light and shadow.

On a spring day the water may be dimpled for another reason: a hatch of insects is taking place. Mayflies, those delicate creatures so relished by trout, have left the stream for their brief aerial existence. Turning their backs on two or three years as flattened nymphs or naiads that can swim like a fish when necessary, they climb up out of the water by the thousands and shed their skins.

It is at this point you may recognize the new adults: gauzy triangular wings held straight up, large compound eyes, and two or more threadlike projections from the abdomen. Soon they will mate, lay their eggs, and die. And *soon* it really is, for many of them live but a day or two after leaving the water. Some may emerge, mate, and die in a single morning.

Such a brief life on land means no further need for a digestive system. Indeed, many adult mayflies do not even have a mouth.

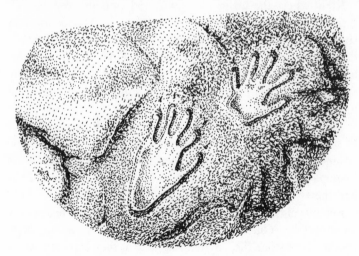

RACCOON PAW PRINTS

MAYFLY

The hollow innards are modified into a sort of balloon, which accounts for the incredible airy lightness of these remarkable insects. When mayflies alight on the water to drop their eggs (some even die before the eggs are laid, so the eggs are liberated when the insect decomposes), the fish rise to snap this floating bonanza. The angler, seeing this performance, tries to find just the right artificial fly to match the hatch.

Right where the water runs swift and smooth over the surface of the rocks you'll find an unusual nursery. Massed together so as to look like dark underwater moss are hundreds of larvae of that biting pest, the black fly. The larvae look like little grubs, attached to the rock by silken webs. Facing upstream, they devour water creatures or tiny algae, some of which are captured in those webs.

The larva grows to full size, then forms a little pupal case. In some species the case is built so as to capture a tiny bubble of air from the rushing waters. Then when the fly emerges from its pupa it pops to the surface in its bubble. The bubble bursts and the fly is catapulted into life.

Remove almost any stone from fresh running water and survey its underside. You'll see flattened insects with sprawling legs: the naiads of stone flies. When full grown, they leave the water and transform into long, dark-colored winged adults. You often see stone flies walking on the snow in late winter. Apparently their dark body color absorbs enough of the sun's heat to allow some species to undertake this final stage of life when most other insects are still asleep.

Your underwater prying will also disclose those little cabin-builders, the caddis worms. Adult caddis flies resemble small brown moths, but with wings held rooflike over the abdomen instead of out flat in the fashion of most moths. Caddis fly larvae are underwater garbage collectors. Looking somewhat like an aquatic caterpillar, the caddis worm cements objects together to form a protective case. Examine it: you'll find it made of sand grains, sticks, or other debris, depending on the species. There the larva lives the balance of its adolescence, dragging the case about wherever it goes. At the first sign of danger it pops back into its shelter—and all the enemy sees is a little tube held to a stone or stick by six tiny feet.

STONE FLY

ADULT CADDIS FLY

Prospectors tell of caddis worms in the Rockies whose cases contained gold nuggets. The best our Vermont species can do is to incorporate a few garnets or black tourmaline crystals into their handiwork. The crunchiness of the structure isn't always a protection, however. The brook trout, for instance, often swallows the caddis worm—case and all.

The brook trout, by the way, is our native species. Brown

and rainbow trout have been introduced into many of our streams. White-edged fins and vermicular (wormlike) markings on the body distinguish the so-called brookie.

Often in September you'll see brookies a foot long or so, working their way into tiny streams so shallow that you can hear the fish splash as they swim upstream. There, in a little gravel bed, they'll lay the eggs that begin a new generation. Thus they are the Vermont counterpart of the salmon leaping its way up a roaring cataract to spawn.

Look for other fish in the Vermont streams: the brook sculpin, for instance, plus the little redbellied and blacknosed dace. The two-inch sculpin darts from place to place in pursuit of water insects and then rests on fins that can spread like little fingers. It's a pugnacious creature and will sometimes do battle with your hands. The dace, less quarrelsome but highly curious, will often nip at your bare toes if you can stand in that chilly water long enough.

Somewhere along its course the brook runs out into a wider, flatter area. Here the waters travel at a less hectic pace. The spot may be where the land levels out, or possibly it is a natural basin filled in by that fur-coated engineer, the beaver.

Beavers often follow brooks and rivers upstream until the water becomes a mere trickle. Somewhere along the way, if conditions are right, the beaver makes its home. Self-sharpening teeth slice through tree trunks and branches as the animal fashions a place to live. Jamming sticks and branches into the mud, the beaver forms the framework of its dam. Lacing more branches, stones, clumps of grass, and armloads of mud together, the beaver will use any material at hand. One time I lost my binoculars during a visit to a beaver pond; I discovered them a couple of years later, securely wedged in the dam—and totally ruined.

Among mammals only the human animal consciously alters its surroundings as much as the beaver. The objective of the beaver is to create a pond deep enough to serve as a pantry for food storage, an underwater entrance for its lodge, and a place of safety. Although it is North America's largest native rodent (one beaver weighed in at ninety pounds), the webfooted creature is slow and clumsy on land. In water, however, it is graceful and well-nigh invincible.

Aspen, or popple, is the beaver's favorite food in Vermont. It stores selected pieces of this and other trees in the mud, to chew on their bark and twigs during the winter. Busy as a beaver, so to speak, it may store more than it can eat. Indeed, it has been said the beaver is like us in another way: it is one of the few living creatures that actually gets fat in winter.

When there are no edible trees or small plants left, the beaver may move to a more bountiful spot, or it may fashion canals and sub-dams back into the woodland. These allow it to forage further afield—and sometimes right into trouble. My neighbor, Nellie Cloe, was delighted with the beavers in a stream near her house until they started a canal in her direction. She viewed their nightly progress with growing alarm as tree after tree succumbed to their advance.

One morning I asked how her beavers were doing. She regarded me accusingly. "And I thought you were my friend!"

In answer to my puzzled look she explained. "You said they'd eat popple and spring flowers and willows and nice things like that. You didn't tell me"—and here she swept a despairing arm toward two freshly-cut stumps on her lawn—"about French lilacs!"

The beaver, of course, is scarcely to blame if we place edible greenery and floodable country roads in the path of progress. Actually, a beaver pond may be a big "plus" for the entire valley. It becomes, in effect, a wooded swamp where a host of living creatures find things to their liking.

Such a pond is often a favorite haunt of shiners and brook trout. The spotted sandpiper patrols its shores, teetering in its peculiar way as it walks along the edge. White-bellied tree swallows and their fork-tailed cousins, the barn swallows, fly just above the water, snapping up gnats and mosquitoes. Knotholes in dead trees make fine nest spots for the tree swallow. The little green heron (actually more blue than green, with chestnut neck and white front) stalks frogs and little fish. Often it assumes outlandish poses as it gets in position for a strike.

Wood ducks nest in nearby hollow trees, some rooted in the water, some on land. Their babies tumble fearlessly to earth shortly after hatching, and obediently waddle after mama to the nearest water. Once, at the edge of a swamp, a female black duck nearly stopped my heart as she flew up from in front of my feet, exposing a dozen white eggs.

Several kinds of snails live in the waters of a swamp or beaver pond. Some have spirally coiled shells—the tadpole snails—while others have shells curled like a ram's horn. The so-called horsehair "snake" often lives a part of its life cycle here, as well. It leaves its insect host where it has grown to maturity and washes down into the stream as a slender whitish worm several inches long. When I was a farm boy we used to believe these Gordian worms, as they are officially called, were horsehairs that came to life when dropped into the water.

HORSEHAIR "SNAKE"

Dragonfly and damselfly nymphs live in those swamps and little ponds. Able to shoot out a hinged lower lip armed at the tip with a pair of pinchers, these creatures stalk and capture anything from a baby fish to smaller members of their own kind. Then, sometimes as much as three years after hatching, they become those familiar colorful insect hawks of brook and swamp.

One time in a West Dover swamp I had set my camera on its tripod for a closeup of a damselfly. It was a pretty creature, with blue wings folded up above its back (dragonflies, by contrast, hold their wings straight out, like an airplane) as it perched on the end of a twig.

The black flies buzzed around my head, and I couldn't help but twitch my nose as one landed dead center. The damselfly saw the motion just as I was ready to press the shutter. It disappeared from the finder, but before I could react it was back again. This time I got a real life picture: a head-on view of a damselfly munching a black fly to bits.

Damsel and dragonflies are found in bogs as well as swamps, but the true bog has a personality of its own. It has many of its own plants and animals, too. When you enter a bog you quickly note the difference—the trees and shrubs and flowers are such as you may not have seen before.

Indeed, you find that you walk differently. This is because each step is a little adventure. Instead of soil and rocks or at least a firm footing, you're treading on a sort of giant sponge. This sponge is made of the remains of leaves and bark and grass and sedges and sphagnum moss—a layer sometimes thirty feet thick or more. And beneath that layer, especially when you're out in the center of the bog, is a pool of coffee-colored water.

A bog usually begins in a spot where water collects and has little or no outlet. Meltwater from a snowy slope may gather in a valley, perhaps, or a natural depression may become filled faster than it evaporates. A number of bogs started at the demise of our last glacier when a great chunk of ice buried in the earth slowly melted and formed a kettle hole. Such a depression becomes filled with stagnant water. This water, surrounded by the plants of the region, receives twigs and leaves, seeds and fruit that drop or roll in from the sides.

Lacking a replacement flow, the water is soon bereft of oxygen as the process of decay uses the available supply of the gas. New material is added but cannot decay either, so it builds up in volume. The result is a thickening mat of organic debris, often known as peat, working in from the edges over countless years.

The soil of such a bog reflects the character of the water, and may be highly acid, thus interfering with the absorption of nutrients by the roots of plants. To get these nutrients, especially nitrogen, which is chemically locked in such a way as to be unavailable, a few plants have turned to their neighbors. These neighbors are the spiders and insects whose bodies contain nitrogen-rich protein.

Your first look at the bog may well show a species especially adapted to this unusual method of feeding: the pitcher plant. A cuplike leaf, lined with downward-pointing hairs, holds a little fluid, including water from a recent dew or rain. Insects, as they wander around the edge of the upright cup, slip or crawl inside. Now begins a desperate struggle. It is easier to slip downward than to climb up those bristly hairs, and the victim slides lower. Eventually it falls to the bottom, is digested by enzymes poured into the water, and the plant gets a little nitrogen.

Look near a pitcher plant for the little sundews. These are roughly the size of half a playing card. They are exquisite little jewels whose leaves bear a number of reddish glistening hairs. Each hair is tipped with a drop of sticky fluid. When an insect lands on the hairs it becomes entangled and enzymes in the leaf soon do away with it.

You'll find other bog plants, all well able to live in those acid surroundings. Bog sedges, belonging to a family of grasslike plants with wiry leaves and triangular stems, are also at home in the dampness. One, the cotton sedge, has a surprisingly large flowering body that looks like an overgrown cotton swab on a drinking straw.

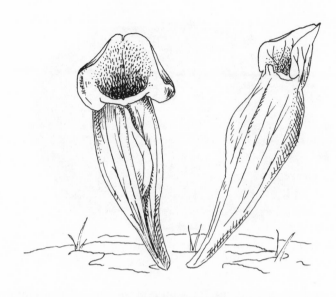

PITCHER PLANT

As you walk through the wettest part of the bog—or place your footsteps, to describe your antics more accurately—you find that each step has its influence on the plants around you. They jiggle and move slightly, as if you and they were all sharing a gigantic waterbed. Jump up and down: the motion sets up a similar tremor that spreads in widening circles, like a ripple on a pond. To me it is always a source of wonder whenever the black spruces, red maples, and willows nod slightly as if condescending to take note of your puny human presence.

Such action is the result of being on a great, loosely-joined raft of vegetation. It's a floating raft, of course, as a group of us discovered once on a bog field trip. We had been seeking the arethusa, or bog pink orchid. Its delicate magenta colors and exquisite petals on top of a six-inch stalk make it one of the bog's rarest treats. And there we were, suddenly, in the presence of not one but *seven* of them.

Hastily I got out my camera. So did several others. There

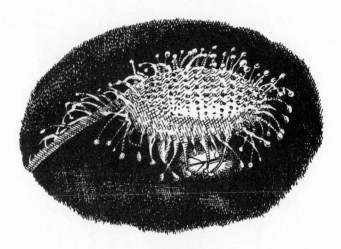

SUNDEW

we stood, a dozen of us, in a little circle around that clump
of orchids. And then an interesting thing happened: the orchids
began to sink. And so did we.

We had long since gotten our legs wet so we didn't notice
what was happening at first. Then somebody realized we were
standing in knee-deep water, whereas moments before it had
been scarcely up to our ankles. This triggered a retreat in twelve
different directions.

The orchids emerged from the water again. Two by two we
gingerly went back and took our photographs. And all around
us everything was shaking. We felt we had about as much sta-
bility as if standing up in a canoe.

More than two dozen orchid species have been found in our
Vermont bogs from spring to fall. At no time or place are they
common and finding any one of them is an occasion. There's
the rose pogonia, for instance, that resembles the orchid in a
corsage, except in miniature. There's also the yellow fringed
orchis and the yellow ladyslipper.

One of the last to bloom presents a dozen or more small white flowers, arranged spirally up the stalk: the lady's tresses. Coming into bloom so late in summer, they seem reluctant to quit the scene. I've seen them bravely poking up through an early snowfall.

LADY'S TRESSES

Where I'd Take You If I Could

Bogs and swamps, marshes and brooks: it's hard to tell, sometimes, where one stops and another begins. It's even hard to define them.

All of these are a part of the watery resource with which Vermont is so abundantly blessed. So, rather than take you at this point to a little brook, say, only to leave when it joins a river, I'll make another suggestion:

Read on.

LAKES AND PONDS

Sprinkled with more than four hundred lakes and ponds, our Green Mountain State is richly blessed with moisture. Take an airplane ride and watch the sun as it is mirrored by waves or placid surfaces below you. There are so many ponds and marshes it's often hard to tell where the water ends and the land begins.

Sharing the thousands of miles of shoreline and billions of gallons of water are more billions of plants and animals. Each could tell an interesting story.

Let's take just one example: the common cattail. Growing from a sturdy rootstock in the mud, it sends up new shoots annually in all directions. In this way a whole cattail marsh may actually be scores of youngsters attached to a single parent—chips off the old block, so to speak.

Each summer the familiar brown cattail develops on the end of its long stalk, fuzzy seeds and all. Later the seeds dance away

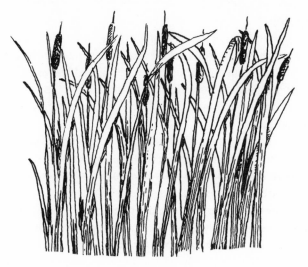

CATTAILS

on their little parachutes, buoyantly adrift in the sunshine. Eventually they drop to earth, perhaps hundreds of miles away. With luck a few of them find a hospitable reception.

This is one way they travel. Another relates to the parachutes themselves. Their silky strands cling to objects, like lint to a sweater. If the parachutes get wet they can become plastered against the shells of turtles or the legs of shorebirds. And thus it may be that a new-dug farm pond suddenly sprouts a crop of cattails: a few seeds might have been carried in by a passing duck or heron.

Cattails were once more highly prized than they are today. The rootstocks were dried and made into flour. The new shoots were cooked like asparagus. The pollen was gathered and used to impart a rich golden taste—if you can imagine such a thing—to hotcakes, breads, and other baked goods. One use I can recommend is to collect a few of the flower spikes in early summer when they're green and about the size of a pencil. Boil them, butter-and-salt them, and you've got a tasty preview of corn on the cob.

Among the bizarre plants along the shore are the bur-reeds, with greenish brown fruit looking like prickly marbles on a stalk. Equally striking in appearance are the pointed leaves of arrowhead, poking out of the water or the mud along the shore. The plant's waxy-white flowers with three petals are borne in groups along the stem.

Arrow-shaped leaves are found also on pickerel weed. This plant's purple flowers, crowded at the top of long spikes, are so short-lived that you usually see only a few good blooms. The rest are in various stages of disrepair.

In deeper water you may see the pond lilies. They are of two main types: white and yellow. Their floating leaves, or lily pads, may reach up from the bottom through more than six feet of water.

Spatterdock, the yellow species, has blooms that last a couple

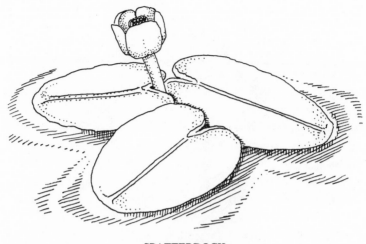

SPATTERDOCK

of days, while the sweet-smelling white lily blooms only a few hours. It usually opens after sunrise and may be closed by mid-afternoon.

One unusual plant often grows along the mudflats or in the shallows. It has relatives that thrive in sandy soils as well, and along parched roadsides. The various species contain silicon, a main ingredient of sand and glass, in their tissues. Matted together, they form a fine abrasive pad; hence they're often known as scouring rushes. The hollow stems of our small scouring rushes are jointed but unbranched. Pull on them and they come apart with an audible pop. In the spring they bear a cylindrical reproductive structure resembling a tiny pine cone. Later they produce coarse, hairlike structures that give them the name of horsetails.

Among the most venerable of higher plants, today's little horsetails can be traced back to ancestors that were full-sized trees in steamy coal age swamps long before the coming of the dinosaurs. Today's beach pine with its long, trailing branches

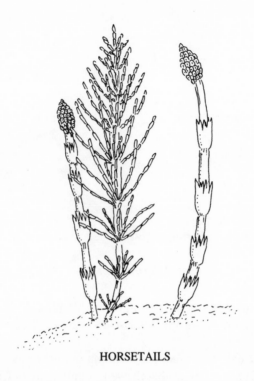

HORSETAILS

grows along warm coastlines on this continent and other parts
of the world: a modern horsetail tree.

Looking down into the shallows you may see a number of
rooted plants. These include such submerged species as round-
leaved and brown-leaved pondweeds, and the pink-flowered
water smartweed with its oval shining leaves floating on the
surface. There's also that favorite aquarium plant, the long-
leaved eelgrass, or *Vallisneria*.

Eelgrass grows firmly rooted to the bottom. Its relative, also
resident in thousands of aquariums, is the dark green *Elodea*,
or brittleweed. The leaves of this plant are in whorls around
a stem that easily breaks into pieces. Each Elodea fragment continues to float about, sometimes sending a long threadlike root

that serves as a slender anchor line. With a storm the line or the stem may break—and away goes the little pioneer on another adventure.

Smallest of all flowering plants are the tiny floating green discs known as duckweed. Sometimes, in a sheltered cove, they cover the water like a blanket. Each plant, scarcely the size of this capital letter "O," has a slender root that hangs down a short ways into the water. There are occasional simple flowers, but they are rare. Almost all duckweeds reproduce by budding new plants from the original.

Lake Champlain has recently played unwilling host to a few Old World species that have arrived and show no tendency to leave. There's the water chestnut, for example, with its floating rosettes of triangular leaves and pyramid-shaped fruits, each bearing four sharp points. Thousands of the plants form solid rafts, preventing swimming, boating, or fishing.

The popular aquarium plant known as myriophyllum, or European milfoil, has escaped its glass tanks and creates long feather-leaved tangles. These will foul propellers and clog the shallows. They create an uncanny sensation as their ten-foot length slithers along the body of a swimmer. I can attest this from experience.

Call this assemblage weeds if you will, but—with the exception of those unwelcome foreign visitors—they're a necessity to the life of the pond. Ducks and geese feed on pondweeds by the ton. Muskrats eat pondweed tubers and cattail rootstocks, and fashion their homes of reeds and rushes and mud. And if you're an angler, you know the Big Ones lurk among the plants. There they wait for the smaller fish to venture from their protective shelter.

Among the animals, one group seldom mentioned in books but often seen in the water is that of the bryozoans, or moss animals. They look somewhat like underwater cantaloupes attached to sticks or rocks. I've seen their colonies, two feet below the surface, in the shallows of Long Point in Ferrisburg.

There are colonies in many other places: Hapgood Pond in Peru, Emerald Lake in Dorset, and quiet areas of some of our larger rivers. A bryozoan colony is firm to the touch, green and spherical and usually about the size of a grapefruit. Like a soft coral (but unrelated) it is made of thousands of tiny individuals whose threadlike tentacles scoop passing edibles from the water.

Bristleworms, aquatic relatives of the familiar earthworm, creep about like their larger cousins. They are vital to the life of the pond. Dead plant and animal material will soon disappear under the onslaught of their little groping mouths and tiny gizzards.

Another relative, the leech, frequents the water for a less commendable purpose, at least to our way of thinking. Gifted with a powerful vacuum-type mouth and posterior sucker, almost any of the various species of leech will attach to a handy part of your body. Then the rubbery creature nips a tiny hole in your skin. Actually, it creates little trouble except to your composure. Leech saliva prevents the clotting of blood. Its essential chemical, hirudin, is still used today in medicine. This explains why a bloodsucker bite may bleed long after you've given the author its comeuppance.

LEECH

The many kinds of pond snails creep along on stones and weeds, rasping away at algae and other edibles with little file-like tongues. Some of them live on a commuting basis, crawling on objects near the surface during the day and retiring to the bottom at night. Others live just the opposite, so your flashlight may show a different snail population after dark than you saw a few hours earlier.

There are snails with a tough operculum that fits the shell opening snugly when the snail has retired, thus shielding it from enemies or drought. Others merely contract the fleshy body for protection. Their pathetic little empty shells can be seen by the thousands on a shore after a pond has dried.

A few snails bear living young while others spread their masses of jellylike eggs on underwater objects. A dozen of the latter from Shelburne Pond ended up as residents in my aquarium. It was fascinating to watch their transparent eggs on the glass as they developed tiny black eyes at the base of stubby tentacles—and then to see the formation of abbreviated shells. The unborn youngsters cavorted in their gelatinous prisons with an alacrity far beyond that of their sober-sided parents.

Snails, with their single shell, are known as univalves. Their two-shelled cousins, the bivalves, include the clams and mussels. If you have a garment with mother-of-pearl buttons, you probably owe such adornment to a freshwater mussel. Occasionally the mother produces the pearl as well; I found a mussel shell gaping open on the shore of Lake Dunmore, complete with three pearls the size of tapioca.

Native Americans used freshwater mussels as food, cooked or raw. The shells were fashioned into spoons or ornaments or beads or wampum. Today we're apt to regard the freshwater mussel merely as a curiosity (which, doubtless, is fine by the mussel). To other people it is just a softbodied mollusc that lives between two ashtrays.

There are freshwater bivalves of several kinds. They range from little fingernail clams as small as a grain of popcorn to the large pearly mussel, nearly four inches long. Through a siphon and filter arrangement they take in water, strain out food organisms, and pass the water out again.

In this manner mussels not only feed but reproduce. The

female receives the sperm of a convenient male nearby and unites them with her eggs. Efficiency, yes—ecstasy, no. The eggs develop into microscopic larvae, called glochidia. In keeping with their unromantic beginning, the female merely squirts them out by the thousands. Away they go, their little shells rhythmically snapping shut and then opening again.

If a rare and lucky snap happens to catch the gills or fin of a fish, the little clam is on its way. Otherwise it will perish. Once attached it becomes embedded in the fish's skin, and grows there for several weeks. Then it drops off, settles down, and becomes merely a stodgy mussel, with little hint of its adventuresome earlier life.

If you have puddled around in the water very long you may have met the common crayfish. This little freshwater lobster can deal a respectable pinch with its claws. Also, like a lob-

CRAYFISH

ster, it can travel faster in reverse than forward, scooting backward out of harm's way.

The female crayfish carries her eggs attached to her abdomen. When the babies hatch there's a unique nursery available. Each youngster holds tight to a swimmeret with its nippers. There it can feed on leftovers from its mother's meal—bits of a dead fish, perhaps, or the remains of an unfortunate snail or insect.

Much smaller and more numerous are the water fleas and water-hoppers. They are enormously important as food for tiny fish and other creatures. Scoop up a jar of pond water and you may find you've captured some of both.

The water fleas look like an undersized tomato seed, or a flea encased in a glassy shell. They capture floating organisms as they cruise through the water. With a magnifying glass you can see right through a water flea—dark eye, digestive system, reproductive organs, beating heart, and all.

WATER FLEA

The water-hopper resembles a miniature lobster without any legs. It rows itself through the water by quick strokes of its long antennae. One abundant type is called cyclops after the monster of Greek mythology. Like its namesake, this tiny hopper has but a single central eye: a ruby red jewel, probably sensitive only to light and dark. The female carries her eggs along her sides, like saddlebags on a horse.

Larger crustaceans, looking a bit like the dry-land sowbugs,

161

are often known as scuds—or, if you want to get technical, amphipods. Scuds are flattened sideways, like a flea, and are gifted with the ability to swim, climb, and jump with about a dozen pairs of legs. These creatures are found in great numbers under driftwood and decaying vegetation. They are not fussy in their eating habits but consume almost anything, plant or animal.

When it comes to mating, the male grasps the female firmly with a clutch that cannot be broken. If not so inclined, however, she can still get away: she summarily sheds her skin. This, I suppose, leaves him with nothing but intentions.

Aquatic naiads of damselfly and dragonfly creep slowly among the submerged stems. There each naiad waits for some small neighbor to venture within reach. Then out shoots that hinged lower lip with its needled pinchers.

The giant waterbug, as much as two inches long, catches its victims with forelegs shaped like a pair of ice tongs. Then it drains their body fluids with a beak that acts like a drinking straw. The female of this species has the interesting habit of laying her eggs on the back of the male. At Cole Pond north of Jamaica, I watched what I thought was a duel between two giant waterbugs. It turned out, however, to be just a female impressing on her mate the joys of parenthood. Finally he succumbed and remained in what seemed to be patient submission while she festooned his back with about a hundred of his future offspring.

GIANT WATERBUG

Luckily, the waterbug has no designs on any human swimmers who might pass by. The only bite I've heard of was received by a lady biologist who impulsively offered her finger to a waterbug in an aquarium. "Well," she said ruefully, holding up a painfully swollen digit, "so much for scientific research."

The water boatmen look like miniature rowboats, each with a single pair of oars. They're active little creatures, darting and rowing ahead of you as you swim or paddle along. When they dive a thin film of air covers their bodies so they look silver underwater. Since this air blanket makes them buoyant, they throw a leg around a submerged object and cling there like a drunk to a lamppost.

The many aquatic beetles are hard to describe—except for two that are easily recognized. One is the dark brown diving beetle, shaped like a prune pit but twice its size. It floats at the surface until a likely looking fish or tadpole swims by. Then it quickly raises its wing covers to admit a bubble, partly closes them to imprison the air, and darts after its prey. Special openings on its back allow it to breathe this bubble for as much as five minutes.

The other predatory beetle is known to almost everybody. This is the shiny black whirligig beetle, whose wild gyrations are seen on almost any pond or swamp. Circling and wheeling faster than the eye can follow, it can also dive or spring into flight if necessary. It has excellent vision, with eyes divided by a horizontal ridge. Thus it has bifocals of sorts, with one half seeing into the air while the other half looks down into the water.

Of course you've met that troublesome fly known as the mosquito. Its active little wigglers spend a couple of weeks in a placid pool. Then they transform into swimming pupae, or tumblers, and thence into adults. The females fly off to add a new dimension to your outdoor experience. The males are no bother at all: they content themselves with the sap of plants and the nectar of flowers.

The mosquitoes' gigantic relatives, the harmless craneflies, begin life as large, wormlike larvae. When adult they look like huge mosquitoes and are often swatted as such. Sometimes they get tangled in spider webs or inside a window, sacrificing a leg or two as they escape.

Doubtless you've also met those small flies known as midges. Their numbers include the persistent little punkies, or no-see-ums. Their larvae swim like tiny snakes in the shallows. They may also find a home in a rainfilled tree hole, a puddle in a weathered rock, or even a discarded can or bottle.

Less troublesome midges can often be seen dancing up and down over a certain spot—and sometimes going along when the spot moves. I recall an inspecting officer who was greatly disliked when I was in the service but who gave our unit one of the most delightful inspections we ever had. It seems a flotilla of thousands of midges had established itself over his head like his own little cloud. Up and down our ranks he traveled that morning—his active personal adornment convulsing everyone but the man directly in front of him.

You'll see but few aquatic mites or spiders. The red water mites crawl on the bottom or swim like pudgy little rice-sized balls, eight legs flailing valiantly as they seek their prey. The diving spiders, looking like their dryland cousins, trap bubbles of air in silken nets held between their legs. They take this air to a larger underwater diving bell, where they eat their food and raise their families.

Among the vertebrate animals, one of the least welcome is the lamprey eel. Actually not an eel at all, it is a slender creature sometimes more than two feet long. With its sucking mouth and rasping teeth it clings to fish and digs its way into their flesh. The lamprey has made its way into Lake Champlain, perhaps by attaching to barges and boats.

The true eels are really fishes built on the extension plan.

MIDGE   AQUATIC MITE

Beginning life in the ocean, they drift toward our shores and follow rivers and brooks as youngsters. They work steadily upstream for months or even years, sometimes going overland on rainy nights.

The males seem to lose the wandering urge first. They are more common in the lower part of the Connecticut River, say, than in its tributaries. If you catch an eel in one of the smaller streams or an upcountry pond it's likely to be a female.

After half a dozen years, more or less, the female heads back to mate and lay her eggs in the sea. Thus she reverses the travel route taken by the salmon, which swims upstream to spawn.

The salmon has been the subject of restocking efforts by Vermont and New York in Lake Champlain for several years. So have lake trout, brown, rainbow, and brook trout in selected lakes and ponds. The Champlain effort has been markedly successful, and anglers have reported good catches in the past few seasons. Last year I watched a great landlocked salmon jump at least twice its length out of the water in the middle of Shelburne Bay. It did this three separate times. Small wonder the scientific name of such a splendid creature is *Salmo*—the leaper.

All these members of the trout family need cool, clean water. In spring they come close to shore, but warmer weather finds them in the depths. Here the water stays colder and—if there's a sufficient oxygen supply—more suited to their needs.

Nowhere near as fastidious is a fish that has been introduced in several lakes and ponds, the common carp. Weighing several pounds, it has large glistening scales and a downpointing mouth with fleshy lips. When mating, it thrashes about in water

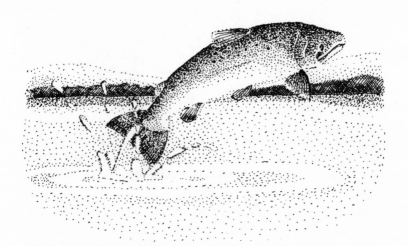

LANDLOCKED SALMON

so shallow its broad back may not even be covered.

The physical results of the presence of carp are impressive. Aquatic vegetation is uprooted and the water is churned until it's little more than liquid mud. Native species quit the scene and head for a better spot—if they can find it. When the carp are spawning in the spring you can hear the uproar before you get to the backwaters of the lake or quiet river where it is all taking place.

Spring fever grips many other fish species as well. Northern pike and pickerel mate and play in the shallows and on the flooded lowlands. This gives rise to an interesting phenomenon: an angler up a tree. From such a vantage point one can see the spawning fish. Your fishing rod is a firearm. A shot close to your target will stun it—and your hunting license has gained you a fish.

Walleyed pike run into the shallows and into river mouths to spawn. Each spring anglers line the banks of rivers along Lake Champlain—the Lamoille, for instance, and the Missisquoi.

There they may stand shoulder to shoulder, in hopes of snagging one of these tasty prizes with the peculiar glassy stare.

Yellow perch, distant relatives of the walleye, drape their strings of eggs among the water plants. The vertical bars on the fish's body, so conspicuous in open water, help it disappear among the swaying stems.

Members of the sunfish family, such as smallmouth and largemouth bass and bluegills plus the spangled little pumpkinseed, clear a gravelly circle on the bottom for their eggs. This spot is patrolled by the male, who fiercely defends his territory against all comers. Many a bass has been taken when it did battle with a passing plug or spinner that drifted close to its home.

The smallmouth bass is found in colder waters, often with gravelly bottoms. The largemouth is more apt to frequent weedy and warmer areas. Both are known as black bass, and are often distinguished by a dark horizontal line running from head to tail. A black bass school may actually consist of one or both parents, keeping a close watch over a hundred or more youngsters. When such a guardian is hoisted aloft on a fishline the waiting predators may move in and destroy half the family before it is reunited.

Family ties are also strong with the common horned pout, or bullhead. This little catfish, black or yellow-brown in color (there are a couple of species), may care for as many as three

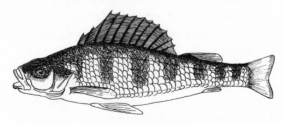

YELLOW PERCH

hundred tiny editions of itself like a shepherd with a flock of sheep. The closely packed youngsters, circling slowly at the same level, look like a wobbly black pancake in the water, attended and urged along by their solicitous parent.

Many members of the catfish family, living as they often do in murky bottom waters, have a singular ability to detect the presence of food. This I've noticed with the half dozen bullheads in residence at my own aquarium. Those long whiskers (barbels) around the mouth are sensitive, of course, but so are other parts of the body. If the fish's side or belly, or even a fin, happens to touch a piece of meat dropped in the tank, the fish will stop at once. Backpedaling and circling, it locates the morsel in an instant.

There are many more fish species in Vermont—upwards of a hundred in all. Largest is the Lake Champlain sturgeon, in the hundred-pound class with its plated hide and underslung jaw. At the other extreme are a dozen and more species of minnows, shiners, and dace. Champlain also has the lake catfish, a large relative of the bullhead, reaching ten pounds or more. In addition, there's the powerful north country muskellunge, plus the portly sheepshead with its peculiar blunt nose and wonderful chowder potential. And there's also the bowfin.

The heavy-scaled bowfin's rounded tail, preceded in the male by a distinctive spot, will help distinguish it from other fish. So does its pugnacious attitude. One spring day I was returning to the access area at the Panton South Slang when a bowfin challenged my canoe paddle, stroke by stroke. This didn't work so it took on the whole canoe. Sure enough, it chased it right out of the water at the loading ramp.

Perhaps you've done a little winter ice fishing. If so, you may have met the six-inch Lake Champlain smelt, whose iridescent coloring and almost perfumy aroma led to its Scandinavian name *smoelt*, the Beautiful One. Scientists say it's an oceanic visitor who came to stay—thus joining the lamprey eel and salmon.

Actually, it's impossible to give an accounting of Vermont fish. An angler may dump a load of live bait at the end of a day on the water, thereby adding to that lake's finny population. A fish may still be alive when it's brought home and given its freedom in the nearest pond. Or, people being what they are, a favorite species may be transported from one area to another in a private propagation program.

Such a do-it-yourself effort paid off better than anybody thought it would at Spruce Lodge Pond, in South Lincoln. Spruce Lodge is on the headwaters of the New Haven River. A few bullhead were introduced behind the beaver dam at the pond. Soon everybody was catching bullpout, as they're called. A few years later the dam broke during a flood. Then, for the rest of the summer, people were hauling in bullhead all down the river. Yet there are few books on fishing that'd venture to suggest you would catch such a fish in a rushing trout stream.

The same might go for the amphibian and reptile populations. You may think of the gravel-voiced bullfrog as a resident of the lily pads and backwaters and you'd be right. But there's at least one shallow farm pond half the size of a tennis court that has a thriving population of Jug-o-Rum, as America's largest frog is also called. I know, because I put a handful of bullfrog tadpoles there ten years ago. Their goggle-eyed grandchildren have been bellowing at the Holsteins and grasshoppers ever since.

So impressive is the bullfrog's voice that a visitor from Nairobi, used to the nightly cries and howls of animals on the African plains, went back to his own country from Whitingham thinking he'd been duped. Those grunts and grumbles from the Harriman Reservoir *must* have been made by something big, he insisted. A wild hog, perhaps, or an animal like it. But a frog with a six-inch body length? Impossible!

BULLFROG

Somewhat similar to the bullfrog but about half its size is the common green frog. Its voice sounds like the plink of a banjo—all on one note.

A much more melodious sound is that of the male American toad. You may hear its long musical trill from a pond or swamp on a night late in May. Soon there will be strings of toad eggs draped on submerged objects and over the bottom—a sign that summer is almost at hand.

The song of a frog or toad is made with its mouth closed. Sometimes it's even produced underwater. That sound is a sort of outsized hum. It's amplified by a resonant throat pouch (toad, treetoad, spring peeper) or expandable sides that puff out with every beep or belch or groan (most other frogs).

You have already met the terrestrial brick-red offspring of the little sulphur-bellied pond salamander, familiar as an adult in almost every lake or pond. It's sometimes called the water lizard, but true lizards have scales and toenails and other reptilian features. Besides, lizards are creatures of much warmer climates than afforded by Vermont.

Among the common aquatic reptiles are two turtles and a water snake. The painted turtle, with smooth olive-colored upper shell and yellow lower shell plus red-streaked limbs and neck, may inhabit almost any pond or marsh. You often see several of them sunning on a log or grassy bank.

Less apt to seek a sunbath is the common snapping turtle. When it comes out on land it is usually for the purpose of finding a spot to lay its eggs. During such a mission it takes a sour viewpoint about anything that gets in its way. A snapper on land is about as friendly as a steel trap.

This gray-brown creature with ample upper shell and skimpy under shell often lays its eggs along roadsides. There, in the gravelly shoulder, the eggs are hatched by the sun. Once, along a highway near Swanton, Peg and I enjoyed a picnic within ten yards of a large female snapper. She paid us no attention as she deposited about twenty leathery white eggs in a hole she made at the edge of the pavement. By fall they'd be ready to produce a new crop of snappers—cheerful disposition and all.

Another reptile, the common water snake, is often wrongly called the moccasin. You may see it basking on a grassy bank or draped on a limb overhanging the water. From there it quickly drops to safety when alarmed.

Beautifully blotched in chestnut, red, black, and cream when young, the water snake frequently becomes dull gray with age.

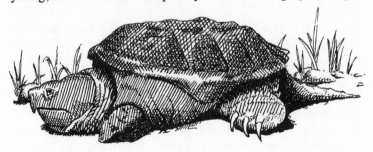

SNAPPING TURTLE

171

Although shy and non-poisonous, it will defend itself savagely when cornered. Mouth open as it lunges, the stout-bodied reptile is the picture of ferocity—and there, unless you're better informed, is your "water moccasin."

To quell any fears, the true water moccasin, or cottonmouth, is seldom found north of Virginia. And, in case you wonder, you will never run afoul of our own water snake while swimming. Superbly alert and agile in the water, it hastily quits the area the minute you come splashing on the scene.

Most shore birds would find a three-foot water snake more than they could handle, but the great blue heron is not above trying. You've probably seen this gangly gray-blue bird: neck crooked in "S" shape, long legs trailing to the rear as it flaps with slow, steady beat on wings that may span six feet in all. Dropping down to the shallows, it stands three feet high—the tallest bird you're likely to see in Vermont.

The great blue, along with the smaller black-crowned night heron (blue gray with white belly) and the brown-streaked American bittern, gain their food by infinite patience. The great blue's long legs allow it to stand in foot-deep water, while the other two often hunt from the shore. Motionless, they await the approach of a meal.

Our larger bodies of water occasionally serve as a stopover for the rare and endangered common loon. Its black head, pointed beak, spotted black-and-white back, white breast, and habit of diving for fish usually will help to distinguish this large bird. Once you hear its voice you'll know it too: a wild, cackling laughter or a long low cry.

The bird isn't crazy as a loon, of course. Yet I recall one evening when four of us were camping at Lake Bomoseen. We were quietly watching our campfire when the night was shattered by that maniacal laughter out in the darkness. We sat without speaking a minute, then did something that made us laugh, too: as at a signal, all four of us got up to put another log on the fire.

172

GREAT BLUE HERON

Vermont's ducks and geese comprise hardly a dozen species but their numbers may run into the thousands. At Dead Creek Refuge in Addison, for instance, a restoration program for Canada Geese has been getting along almost too well. The great gray-brown birds with black head and neck plus white chin strap have multiplied from a few captive individuals to an annual population of hundreds. Thousands more join them during migration.

Such a state of affairs is fine if you like geese. If you're trying

COMMON LOON

to raise corn or other crops you may have second thoughts. Luckily, a wobbly balance has worked out fairly well. Now, not only the skies of western Addison County but those of many other parts of Vermont play host to those great flying "V" formations.

Sometimes along the Champlain and Connecticut River basins the ground may be white with an unseasonal snowfall as hundreds of migrating snow geese alight to rest or feed. White with black wingtips, these birds may blanket the ground as they pause on the way to or from their arctic breeding grounds.

As with the Canadas, snow geese are usually quiet on the ground. In flight, however, they honk and cackle like an unearthly flock of chickens. One time, as we drove through the Missisquoi Refuge near Swanton, the car suddenly developed a horrendous clanking squeal. It sounded as if ten fan belts were slipping and a wheel was coming off. Alarmed, I cut the engine—but the racket continued. In a moment half a thousand snowys flew over us at rooftop level and settled down in a grainfield.

The several duck species in Vermont are of two main groups: the dabblers and the divers. Sneak to the edge of many a pond and you'll most likely see the dabblers, or shallow-water spe-

MALLARD

cies. These kinds feed, tail-up, near the shore. Most familiar of these is the mallard.

The male mallard has an iridescent green head, natty white collar, chestnut breast, and light gray sides. His mate is less colorful—streaked brown and white, like some kind of paddle-footed sparrow.

Their cousin, the black duck, is also streaked, dusky—and extremely wary. Indeed, if you get close enough to see streaks with the naked eye, it's probably a lady mallard.

Smaller cousins of the blacks and mallard are Vermont's two teals—known as bluewinged or greenwinged from the colorful wing patches as they fly. The greenwing's reddish head has a greenish ear patch; the bluewing has a white crescent in front of the eye.

Small and colorful, too, is the handsome wood duck, with swept-back crest and body colors of iridescent green, maroon, and white. It's the wood duck for whom those nest boxes are placed on poles at the edges of swamps and ponds.

Diving ducks find their living in deeper water. If you think a dabbling duck walks funny, contemplate the waddle of a diving duck. Its legs are placed well back to help drive their owner far below the surface. A diving duck has to stand nearly bolt upright to keep from falling on its face. To get very far on land it has to take aim, then stagger forward like your little cousin Fracas taking those first steps.

The identification of diving ducks can cause anything up to fisticuffs among hunters and birders. No little book such as this can settle such an argument. We'll just take a quick look at kinds most apt to be seen.

The canvasback, occasionally seen on large lakes, has a red head and dark beak. True to its name, the back and sides are colored like an off-white, faded tent.

A light body is also found on the scaup duck, but the beak is azure-colored. This gives it the descriptive common name of bluebill.

The goldeneye is somewhat similar except that its sides are snow white, and there's a round white spot in front of the eye. That eye, as the name implies, is a striking golden yellow—in case you're ever close enough to see it. The striking white wing patch is more of a help, but may come too late: it's visible only as the goldeneye takes flight.

As you scan the waters you may see a shaggy-headed duck with slender bill, dark-and-light coloration, and the disconcerting habit of diving just as you're getting a good look. This is most likely a merganser, or fish duck. True to its name, it selects an active, finny meal rather than the stodgy worms, snails, and plant material sought by its broad-billed cousins.

The descriptions of most of these ducks on the past pages have been of male ducks. Don't be too harsh on me, however: their mates are largely brown or gray or streaked and mottled,

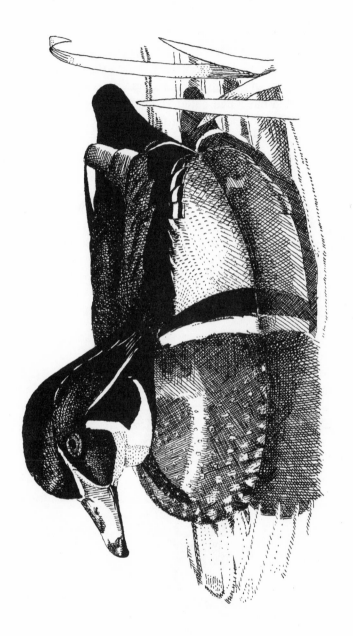

WOOD DUCK

177

as befits their camouflage role on the nest. It's often hard to identify a female all by herself; much easier if she's with an appropriate member of the opposite sex. A lady duck, it seems, is often known by the company she keeps.

Also webfooted but much better flyers are the gulls. Gray wings plus white head and tail identify the common ringbilled gull and its much rarer cousin, the herring gull. The ringbill has matching black spots on upper and lower beak that seem to make a ring near the tip. This is the gull that's often seen by the dozens on plowed fields and meadows.

The larger herring gull has a red spot on the lower bill or mandible, as does its still larger (and still rarer) cousin, the greater black-backed gull. The mottled young of these three species are hard to tell apart for the first two or three years of life. Males and females look alike too—except to each other, I guess, as there always seem to be plenty of gulls.

HERRING GULL

Little brothers to the gulls, so to speak, are those fork-tailed birds known as terns. There are many species worldwide, but the one you're most apt to see in Vermont is the black tern. Its color is almost uniformly gray (white under tail) with black head. It is found in the Lake Champlain area in the summer, notably at Addison's Dead Creek and the Missisquoi refuge. The much lighter (almost pearly gray) common tern can sometimes be seen around St. Albans Bay.

About the only bird remotely like the black tern is the purple martin. This large, dark-colored swallow is often found around water, but usually nests high in those many-holed martin boxes people put up on their lawns. Most terns nest on the ground.

You've already met a couple of sandpipers along the river's edge. There are about a dozen others, but telling them apart can be tricky. It's best for now, perhaps, to say that a small brownish shorebird with long legs and bill is most likely a sandpiper.

Much more easily identified is that bird of glossy black plumage and scarlet epaulets—the redwinged blackbird. The female is heavily streaked, like a large sparrow. She nests in any grass clump or bush, from marshland to meadow.

Usually a welcomed visitor when it returns to Vermont in the spring, the bird is viewed less happily in some other states. Redwings by the thousands may descend on a cultivated field, stripping the plants and ruining the stalks. In some places their loud clamor may make sleep difficult, and a flock settling down in a tree may actually break the branches.

Redwings are sometimes panicked by the marsh hawk or northern harrier. With a wingspan approaching four feet, the harrier courses low over the swamps and meadows. It flies with wings upraised, scanning the ground just below for frogs or mice. You may spot its conspicuous white or yellowish rump even before you see the bird, as its gray or brown body, narrow wings, and long tail seem to blend with the marsh grass.

REDWINGED BLACKBIRD

Nowhere near as common is the osprey. Once nearly every pond and river had its fish hawk but now the bird is seldom seen. Indeed, it is on the endangered species list. A whitish head and underside, brown upper parts, and impressive (up to six feet) wingspan will identify the osprey. So will its habit of flying with wings slightly crooked, plus its spectacular dives into the water.

Scaly fringes on the feet help the osprey cling to a slippery fish. Sometimes the bird gets carried away in its optimism, how-ever, and strikes a fish too heavy to lift. Then it must tow it to shore, struggling every inch of the way, while the fish is doing the same underwater.

Still more rare is our national emblem, the bald eagle. White head and tail, contrasting with its dark body, are known by even a school child, but few of us are lucky enough to see the bird. Yet it is native to Vermont, and I usually sight one or two a year. Be prepared for an impressive bird when you spot one. Its great wings may span seven feet or more. The wings are held flat when soaring; not tilted upward like those of the turkey vulture or the low-flying marsh hawk. Nor are they bent at the wrist like the wings of the osprey. The white head and tail are seen only on adult birds; the juveniles are a blotchy brown the first two years.

Eagle and osprey often sit on a high perch at the edge of the water. While the osprey hurtles headlong after a fish—often after hovering a few moments in the air—the bald eagle snatches its prey with its talons, generally at the end of a long power glide. Sometimes it gets its food second hand by diving at an osprey struggling homeward with a fish. The osprey drops its prize and the eagle swoops to catch it deftly in midair.

As for Vermont's aquatic mammals, you met most of them in our last chapter. Almost all of these animals may find a home in our ponds and lakes, but the muskrat seems especially suited to placid bodies of water. Somewhat smaller than a large house-cat, it dwells among the reeds and cattails. There it digs tubers, cuts new shoots, and feeds on almost anything in the plant line.

Nor is it above a taste of animal protein on occasion. You can often find a muskrat pantry where it has hauled freshwater mussels onto the shore. Dried and baked in the sun, the luck-less molluscs gape open—and a furry little epicure dines on mussel on the halfshell. A muskrat house is a domed structure of reeds and mud and the leftovers from previous meals. A

OSPREY

marsh or shallow pond may be dotted with such homes. Like the beaver, the mushrat, as it's often called, sometimes makes canals or tunnels in a meadow or streambank. If it gets into a farm pond it may tunnel through the dam. This could flush out everything at once, dislodging the muskrat and disgruntling the farmer.

In a conversation about Vermont lakes and ponds it's usually not long before someone brings up the subject of the Lake Champlain monster. Dubbed Champ, he's been discussed, argued about, poo-poohed, and made the star of innumerable stories. There are books about Champ, songs about Champ, and poems about Champ. Port Henry, New York, on Champlain's western shore, even has a statue of him.

And just what may this creature be, anyway? A basking sturgeon, several feet long with its scaly back just breaking the surface? A raft of those diving ducks, bobbing out there among the waves? A whole school of fish, playing and jumping and creating a general commotion?

How unromantic. Much more exciting to consider Champ as related to the Loch Ness monster, perhaps—whatever that may be. Then there's the thought that he could be the latest in a long line of descendants from the days of the dinosaurs.

Or could the elusive creature be a survivor from the time when the arm of a great ocean once covered the Champlain area? After all, some of the world's oldest coral reefs can be found today in the Colchester region. There's genuine beach sand in Castleton and on the bluffs just south of Burlington. And the lake has plenty of water to hide almost any sea creature—as much as four hundred feet in places. A whale skeleton was unearthed in Charlotte—could Champ possibly be some form of landlocked whale? There's something wrong with almost every suggestion, yet the tales persist.

A few benighted souls, gifted with little imagination and no spirit of adventure, have even suggested the dark form is none other than a "marching wave." Apparently caused by wind or currents, such a ridge of water advances steadily across the lake, far from any vessel large enough to have caused it. One such wave, about two feet high, rocked our boat near Thompson's Point in Charlotte and continued south until it was lost from view. From a distance such a disturbance could easily appear like the back of a sea serpent.

And what do *we* say as to the identity of the much-discussed monster of Lake Champlain? Let me answer with an account of what happened one summer day.

Peg and I had been enjoying a sunny afternoon in our sailboat near Panton where Champlain is nearly two miles wide. The wind died after a while, and we found ourselves becalmed in the middle of the lake. So we sat and drowsed in the sun, waiting for a helpful breeze. Then we curled up in the bottom and fell asleep.

We were both awakened by a tremendous noise near the boat. Splash!

My wife found her voice first. "Good heavens! I'm glad they didn't drop *that* anchor in our boat!"

I agreed. From the sound it would have taken us down with it.

We lay there a few minutes, waiting to hear the rattle of a chain, perhaps, or the creak of a boom swinging on a mast, or even the sound of voices. But nothing.

Finally our curiosity would wait no longer. We both sat up at once. But in every direction from our boat the lake was empty for nearly a mile. We were alone on the water.

What made the disturbance? A humungous fish? Something dropped from an airplane high overhead? Or could it have been the elusive Champ?

Many people have reported seeing the Champlain monster. Others have even produced photographs to prove it. They've described a humped back, long neck, or a fin or flipper waved in the air.

Peg and I can lay no claim to such sightings or photographs. Other people may know how it looks or how long it is, true. But if and when the Lake Champlain monster is finally brought up from the deep we can say with confidence that we already know the sound it makes.

Splash!

Where I'd Take You If I Could

The Northern Cloverleaf. By now you may have gathered that almost any tour through Vermont will be well worth the trip. You're right, too. There'll be plenty of variety and a sense of something new around almost every corner. About the only thing lacking will be boredom.

Take, for example, the Northern Cloverleaf. It's especially placed at the end of our chapter on water, yet along the way you'll see roadsides in bloom, lofty mountains, quiet woodlands, and farms going back to nature. Indeed, the 275-mile junket could fit almost any of our chapters.

It fits just about every road condition, too, in its circuit through six of Vermont's fourteen counties—from bustling modern highway to quiet gravel byway.

You may wish to plan two days for this tour. We'd suggest the large (easternmost) loop the first day. The second day's wanderings can cover the rest and take you back to your starting place. Or you could take each of the circles as a separate trip entirely.

Begin by heading east on U.S. Route 2 out of Montpelier. Look for ringbilled gulls over the Winooski River to your left. These birds can be found hundreds of miles inland, even if we do call them seagulls.

Shortly after crossing the river bear to your left onto Route 14 at East Montpelier (about six miles from town). Soon you're winding through pastoral countryside, with low mountains to your right, hills to your left, and farmland all around. North Montpelier is three miles further, complete with its little pond (right) and fishing access area if you care to stop.

You're now following the Kingsbury Branch of the Winooski River. This stream comes down through East Calais from Sabin Pond ("Woodbury Lake," the fishing access sign says) three miles further north.

186

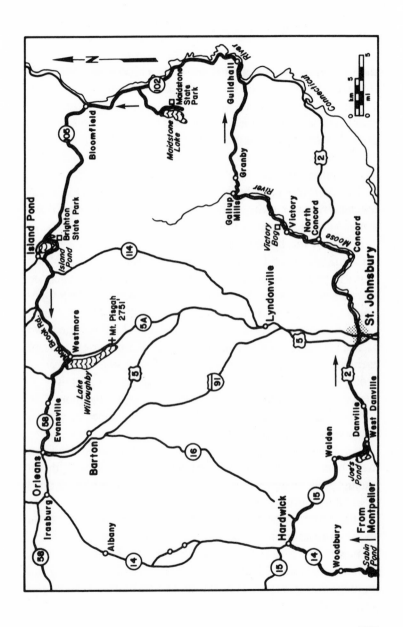

187

On you go, past Sabin Pond, through Woodbury and alongside swamps with cattails and reeds and redwinged blackbirds in summer. At nearly twenty-four miles is a little pipe on the right, running cool water into a tub from a hillside spring above. It makes a handy place to rest for a few minutes.

The road continues, up and down, curving as a country road should, to the town of Hardwick. Running through the center of Hardwick is the Lamoille River; turn right (east) out Route 15 and follow the river two miles until it veers to the north (left) along Route 16.

The river may veer, but you do not. Stay on Route 15. Sugar maples grow along this hilly valley; now and again you'll see a sugar house, complete with its little cupola for the escape of steam from the boiling sap.

Continue east and south on Route 15 through Walden. Two miles beyond this town you're alongside Joe's Pond, named after an early native American resident. Now, at West Danville, you rejoin U.S. Route 2. Tricky traffic here: watch it!

A scant three miles further east on Route 2 is the little town of Danville, site of the annual Dowsers' Convention. There, each September, people gather from as far away as Australia— brought together by their interest in the ancient art of dowsing. At one of these meetings I learned you can dowse for more than water. You can seek hidden treasure, for instance, or a good location for your new home. You can even search for oil. Nor are you always confined to the use of a forked stick. You can use a bent rod that swings sideways instead of dipping down like the stick when on location. You may also use a pendulum, or even a carefully-held blade of grass.

After leaving the village green of Danville, Route 2 takes you about ten miles further to St. Johnsbury. As you come onto South Main Street you're but two blocks from one of New England's famous museums. Housed in a carved red sandstone building on the right (east) side of Main Street, the Fairbanks Museum and Planetarium is a storehouse of natural history. Open from 10 A.M. to 4 P.M. (Sundays 1 P.M. to 5 P.M.), the museum contains a wealth of specimens from Vermont and around the world. There's a fifty-seat planetarium and the Northern New England Weather Observatory, plus hands-on science exhibits. Peg and I have spent many hours there—and we'll never see it all.

After your visit there (tell them I said "hello"), continue on Main Street another block and turn downhill on Maple. Turn right at the bottom of the hill onto U.S. Route 5 (Railroad Street). Get in the center lane at once and turn left (east) back onto familiar U.S. Route 2—now called Portland Street.

Continue east over the Passumpsic River past shops and stores. The Maple Museum is on your right about three-quarters of a mile from the bridge. Just before the Maple Museum you cross one of the Passumpsic's tributaries, Moose River.

Tumbling over rocks and ledges, but less boisterous further upstream, the Moose River will be your companion for the next sixteen miles. You cross it twice on Route 2, traveling through second growth trees a few dozen years old.

Just beyond East St. Johnsbury the road takes you through a stand of evergreens, most of which are white pines. Continue on through the little village of Concord, past mixed hardwoods and evergreens, to a blacktop road that turns off to your left, at North Concord. This road goes to Victory, Gallup Mills, and Granby.

Now, about eleven miles east of St. Johnsbury, you are headed into some wild country. Out west it'd be six-shooter territory; here you may want your camera for shooting of another kind. Look for deer or bear or moose—or even the rare gray jay if you're interested in birds.

The blacktop turns to gravel. It winds three miles through woods and open land to the hamlet of Victory, identified by a couple of buildings and an abandoned school. Above this point the Moose River wanders through lands of alder and red maple, willow and marsh plants: the famous Victory Bog.

Nearly three miles beyond Victory a large boulder on the left bears a bronze tablet in memory of Fred Mold. Fred worked tirelessly to preserve this wild area so it wouldn't become a reservoir, perhaps, or a corridor for a large power project. The unmoving boulder and the arching trees that shelter it give quiet testimony to this man who once told me "there are plenty of ideas for a big 'wasteland' like this. I have an idea, too: why not just let it be?"

Half a mile beyond the Fred Mold memorial, Bog Brook comes in from the left to join the river. There's a parking lot nearby. Following a path from the parking lot to your left along a soggy abandoned railroad embankment you may go a short distance into the bog. Along the way you stand a good chance of seeing moose or muskrat, bog orchid or beaver.

Four miles beyond the Bog River bridge and its parking lot, turn right at the town of Gallup Mills. The road starts optimistically here as blacktop but runs out of enthusiasm in a scant half mile. Soon you're clattering along on gravel again through the woods to the town of Granby.

After four more winding miles you catch a glimpse of the cliffs of New Hampshire, ahead of you and across the Connecticut River. Around you are woods that sound (and look) colorful, with some of the trees known by the tint of their bark: black cherry, yellow birch, gray or American beech, and white birch. A few more miles and you'll drop down to Guildhall (pronounced with the "d" silent) and Route 102.

Turn left (north) onto 102 into Guildhall. Now the Connecticut River is on your right and, beyond it, New Hampshire. In half a mile or so you're in a white pine forest. Further on, these pines are joined by white birches on both sides of the river.

About eleven miles north of Guildhall a gravel road turns left off 102 to Maidstone Lake. The lake's clear waters and forested shores are well worth the visit. Lake trout and landlocked salmon live in the cool depths and there are facilities for campers and vacationists at Maidstone State Park.

When the gravel road to the lake appears to fork (at about two miles) take the left fork. The road to the State Park and campground leads along the left (east) side of the lake. Here's a good chance to become familiar with the yellow birch: the lakeshore road goes through an almost-pure forest of this tree with the shiny bronze bark and the wintergreen-smelling twigs.

After enjoying the park and the forest, retrace your steps to Route 102. Turn left (north) and, five miles later, left again on Route 105. You're alongside the Nulhegan River with little tributary brooks joining it from the highlands to the north.

Open land and abandoned farms alternate with mixed woodlands and patches of evergreens. Many of these are spruce and fir. You can often tell the two apart by the slight whitish cast to the foliage of the fir.

Fifteen miles along Route 105 there's a turnoff to the Brighton State Park, a few hundred yards beyond the Ethan Allen Furniture plant. Approach this turn warily: it's on the left (south) and on a little curve. Usually there's not much traffic but having said this I can guess what *your* experience will be.

Brighton State Park has a fine beach. There are nature trails, good camping facilities, and a lovely view north across Island Pond to the town of the same name. It's good for a short stop, a picnic, or—if you've dawdled along the way and happen to have a tent or recreational vehicle handy—a place to spend the night.

Perhaps you wish to pass some time at the town itself. The road continues beyond the State Park and curves toward those spires and buildings you saw from the south end of the lake. Turn right on Route 105 and go back to the town. Here you may pause for an hour—or overnight, if you feel like it.

Continue, today or tomorrow, on Route 105 west. Route 114 turns south about two miles out of town, but stay on Route 105 a little longer.

About one and a half miles west of that Route 114 turnoff is the site of a beaver pond on your right. As you contemplate the work of America's largest native rodent, consider its importance to the fur trade that opened up our wilderness. Consider, also, that beavers were once trapped nearly to extinction: indeed, they were actually imported in hopes they'd not be gone forever. They've done wonderfully well—as many a farmer will agree at the top of his voice as he surveys a flooded hayfield.

Nearly two miles beyond the beaver dam (or four miles from the Route 114 junction in case you missed the pond), take the blacktop road (Hudson Road) to the left. In half a mile turn left again onto gravelly Mad Brook Road.

This road is not as grim as it sounds, but if you'd rather stick to pavement, continue straight on Hudson Road. Then, when you strike Route 5A, turn south (left) to Westmore. We'll meet you there.

Mad Brook Road, easily passable by auto, is a delightful drive up and down through quiet woods and alongside the brook that gives it its name. After a mile the road forks—twice within a stone's throw. In both cases take the right fork. You climb past white cedars with their flattened sprays of yellow-green foliage, then your road wanders along into the open fields.

Shortly the terrain levels off. You're now north of one of Vermont's loveliest jewels, Lake Willoughby.

As you begin the descent toward the lake, notice the massive boulder in the field to your right. This glacial erratic, a reminder of the last ice age, is a local landmark and a sentinel standing guard over the valley below.

The road takes you down into the town of Westmore, at the north end of the lake. Turning right (northeast) along Route 5A, you're alongside the water's edge. North Beach is worth a stop to enjoy the view and, perhaps, a picnic.

The fifteen hundred-foot cliffs of Mount Pisgah, at the far end of the lake on its east side, are home to a family of the magnificent peregrine falcon. This feathered bullet, able to knock a crow out of the skies, has faced near-extinction since the days of DDT. Now, at last, its fortunes have taken a shaky turn for the better. It has even nested in artificial cliffs elsewhere: high on a hotel ledge in Salt Lake City, for instance, where it spreads daily terror among the resident pigeons.

After your Lake Willoughby visit, continue two miles west to the junction of Route 58. As you go left on 58, you can see Jay Peak Ski Area rising some twenty miles ahead. Closer by, as you pass through Evansville, you're accompanied here and there by the Willoughby River with its falls and rapids and water-worn rocks.

Just before the town of Orleans a sign near this river (at a bridge on your right) proclaims these are spawning waters, closed to fishing from April 7 to June 1. It's a popular spring pastime to watch the rainbow trout as they travel upstream to lay their eggs.

The Orleans area, about 155 miles from your start in Montpelier, is another overnight possibility. Several towns are nearby. The largest is Newport, on Lake Memphremagog (with its legendary furbearing trout), ten miles north on I-91. Camping facilities are also available at Lake Elmore State Park, about thirty-five miles south of Orleans, near Morrisville. Or, for that matter, Montpelier is within another hour's drive south (see Hardwick paragraph, page 195).

Route 58 turns sharp right at Irasburg, four miles beyond Orleans, but your turn will be left (south) on Route 14 at this point. You're on another winding country road, following the waters of the Black River to the village of Albany.

Three and a half miles beyond Albany bear left on the blacktop road toward Craftsbury. Along the way you'll get a glimpse

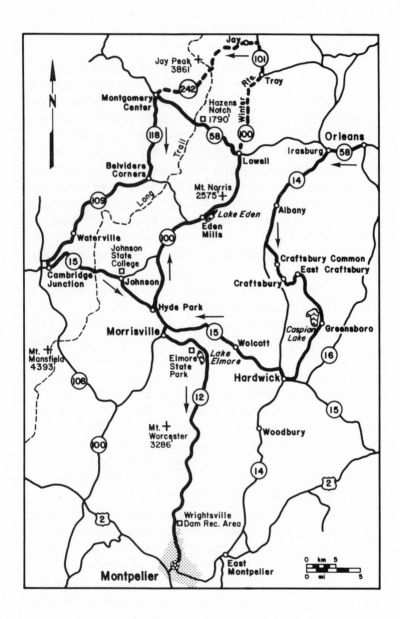

of 4,393-foot Mt. Mansfield, Vermont's highest peak, to the southwest.

Soon you enter that much-photographed town of Craftsbury Common. There you may wish to stop to enjoy the neat little buildings and fences, plus children playing near the bandstand on the grass of the large common. Continue another scenic mile to Craftsbury, with more delights for the photographer.

A mile down the hill take a left to East Craftsbury. There, turn right and continue to Greensboro past one or two maple orchards with their sugar houses. At Greensboro, bear right past the public beach at the south end of sparkling Caspian Lake. Follow this road with its many viewpoints down to Route 16 in Hardwick.

Hardwick is about twenty-five miles north of Montpelier. If you wish, follow Route 14 south, thus retracing the beginning of the large 185-mile loop. Otherwise, continue northwest out of Hardwick on Vermont Route 15.

Route 15 follows the Lamoille River eleven miles to Morrisville. Willows and alders and cattail swamps often mark the river's path. Note the unique wooden structure to your left about three miles west of Hardwick: a covered bridge for the St. Johnsbury and Lamoille County Railroad.

After the road continues through Wolcott, it's flanked by red pines on both sides. This gives another chance to identify this tree. As Route 15A branches off your route toward Morrisville, you can see Mt. Mansfield, now about fifteen miles ahead. Continue on Route 15 about four miles west to Hyde Park; then north (right) on Route 100.

The highway winds onward to Eden Mills. There's a fishing access at Lake Eden on the right (east) and near it a road to the large Mt. Norris Boy Scout Reservation. Mt. Norris itself is three miles ahead off to the left.

At Lowell, about six miles north of Lake Eden, take Route 58 to the northwest. This road starts as blacktop but subsides after a mile into a good gravel surface—in the summer. In winter go straight ahead to Troy, continue north (left) on Route 101 for three miles; then left again on Route 242 through Jay and west to Montgomery Center, where this loop continues.

Route 58, headed west from Lowell, passes through quiet stands of that community of trees familiar to foresters as "b-b-m"—beech, birch, and maple. The road crosses the Long Trail at Hazen's Notch, 1,790 feet above sea level.

One time we surprised a porcupine sampling a tasty shrub along this roadside. When we stopped, the placid rodent gazed at us, bleary-eyed. Then it turned and sauntered off, its quills faintly rattling with each step. It sounded as if Old Quillpig was wearing paper underwear.

The little gravel road comes out into the open with a good view of Jay Peak, about five miles north. The road turns to blacktop and ends at Route 118 at Montgomery Center. A turn to the left (south) on this state road takes you past two little covered bridges in the first mile or so.

In about five miles there's a delightful picnic spot on the right. Shaded by trees, this little area is alongside the South Branch of the Trout River. After a pause here, continue four miles farther to Belvidere Corners; turn right on Route 109.

Route 109 wanders through the valley of the North Branch of the Lamoille River. Back and forth across the stream you go, passing three little covered bridges along the way to Waterville. Turn left on an unnumbered road about three and a half miles south of Waterville, through another covered bridge over the Lamoille River to Route 15 and Cambridge Junction at its far end.

Years ago we drove through one of these wood structures while the car radio was playing. When we came out the other end, four-year-old Janice was puzzled. "What's wrong?" she asked. "Is the radio busted?"

We considered her question. The answer, of course was that

a wooden structure does not interfere with radio waves as steel girders do. Janice, having noted that the radio didn't fade as it did on most bridges, decided it was "busted."

Turning left (east) on Route 15 at the end of that covered bridge you'll be back at Hyde Park in about ten miles. On the way you might like to drive up on the hill at the State College in Johnson. There you'll have one more lovely view—the icing on the cake of this section of the northern cloverleaf.

Turning south on Route 100 from Hyde Park, you're closing the third loop of the coverleaf. At Morrisville, take Route 12 south for five miles to Lake Elmore and the Elmore State Park. This is a favorite vacation area, with many facilities for camping, fishing, and nature study.

Route 12, meandering down past Elmore, is soon joined by the North Branch of the Winooski River. About eight miles south of Elmore a picnic area near a bridge allows a stop opposite Mt. Worcester, some three miles to the west.

The road passes open fields, farms, and woodlands. As you gaze at Vermont evergreens, consider that the largest of these are often white pine. A tall white pine or two graces the dooryard of many a Vermont home.

Mature white pines are apt to be the most wide-spreading of our needle-bearing trees, with the span of the longest branches sometimes more than half the height of the tree. The upper portions are distinctive, too: they're usually bushier than the pointed steeple-tops of most other evergreens in the area.

About four miles south of Worcester is the Wrightsville Dam Recreation Area. Picnicking, swimming, and fishing are popular here for day use, but there are no facilities for a longer visit. I guess this latter condition is acceptable, both for you and for the little tributary of the Winooski River that has been your companion for the past twenty miles or so. The two of you will be at the end of your journey at Montpelier in just about six miles.

The Champlain Islands. The Champlain Islands loop is a much shorter drive than the northern cloverleaf. It spans only about a hundred miles over the extreme northwestern portion of Vermont. This round trip puts you next to our country's sixth largest freshwater lake. It begins on Interstate 89, wanders nearly to Canada, and returns on U.S. Route 7.

North out of Burlington, take I-89 to Exit 17 (the Champlain Islands exit) west onto U.S. Route 2. This spot is known as Chimney Corner. You'll meet it again on the return trip.

About two miles west of Chimney Corner Route 2 crosses the Lamoille River, and you're shortly in the Sand Bar Wildlife Management Area plus Sand Bar State Park. Keep an eye out for turtles crossing the road as you go; they come out of the swamps to lay their eggs.

As I've said before, these unhurried creatures are losing their battle with the automobile. A turtle on the highway, faced with an oncoming car, pulls into its shell—which helps not at all. If you wish to rescue such a creature, remember to place it on the side toward which it was crossing. Otherwise it'll turn around as soon as you're gone and head in that direction anyway.

The Sand Bar swamps to your right and left hold much more than turtles. Tall reeds and buttonbush, growing along the edge, may shelter wild ducks and geese. You may be lucky enough to see a wood duck fly into one of the nest boxes put up on poles in the marsh.

A great blue heron may stand sentinel watch on a point of land or half-sunken log. Muskrats swim in these waters, as do many kinds of fish. Indeed, it's rare not to pass several anglers trying their luck just a few feet away from the roadside.

Sand Bar State Park is one of the popular daytime use areas in all of Vermont. It has a fine sandy beach, good fishing, picnic grounds, and expansive views across the water north and south. Poke along the water's edge; you may find freshwater mussels

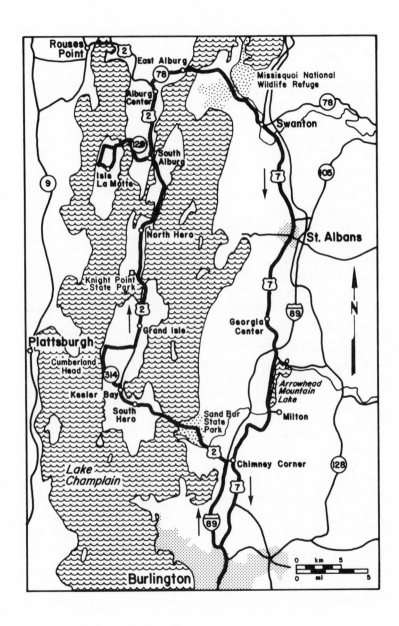

washed up on shore, along with fragments of water weeds that might be just what your goldfish at home need. (Remember, by the way, not to dump a fish tank or its contents—plant or animal—into any native body of water. This may be how populations of carp and that weedy pest, myriophyllum, got started).

Crossing the Sand Bar bridge and more of the narrow causeway, you enter the town of South Hero, at the south end of the island of Grand Isle. South Hero and its companion village of North Hero, about a dozen miles up the road, are named in honor of those two early Vermont partriots, Ira and Ethan Allen.

Route 2 continues north, skirting Keeler Bay. About two miles along this bay shore, just before a boat access to the lake, Route 314 turns west (left) toward the New York ferry.

Follow 314 to the western part of the island. On this three-mile detour you get wonderful views across the lake toward New York's Cumberland Head and the city of Plattsburgh beyond Valcour Island to your southwest. And don't forget to scan those waters for a glimpse of Champlain's resident monster.

When Route 314 circles right again and joins Route 2, turn left (north) toward the town of Grand Isle. Just north of town on the right is the oldest known log dwelling in America, the primitive Hyde cabin, built in 1783. It's open daily until 5 P.M. in the summer—a great place to abandon your horseless carriage and consider the good old days.

Leaving Grand Isle and crossing The Gut by means of a little drawbridge, Route 2 continues to the island of North Hero. Knight Point State Park at the water's edge is a popular camping and fishing spot. This is a good place to look for an osprey, or fish hawk, hovering above the water or plunging down for its lively dinner. Angular wings flexed at the wrist, plus black-and-white facial markings, help distinguish this rare bird from the gulls.

Continue north, enjoying more lakeshore scenery, through

the town of North Hero. The road crosses the narrows of Alburg Passage into South Alburg. Here, if you wish, you may bear left for a loop of about ten miles around Isle La Motte, off to the west.

About five miles beyond South Alburg, leave U.S. Route 2 just north of Alburg Center and turn right on Route 78—unless you wish to continue on Route 2 across the toll bridge to Rouses Point, New York, and a mile north to Quebec, just to touch base as long as you're this close.

Route 78 travels alongside Mud Creek Waterfowl Area. Swampy clumps of alders, willows, buttonbush, red maples, rushes, and cattails give shelter here to many kinds of nesting birds.

Scarcely three miles from Canada at East Alburg, Route 78 crosses a neck of the lake at Sandy Point. The road soon begins a southeast trend, passing through the marshy land and along the river of the Missisquoi National Wildlife Refuge.

We usually stop at Refuge Headquarters on the right (west) to find what birds and animals have been spotted recently. Behind the headquarters building is an entranceway to two nature trails. A pamphlet, available at the start, helps identify features along the way: trees and small plants, the work of beavers, and a peek into the past history of this fascinating area.

South once more, Route 78 joins U.S. Route 7 at Swanton. Pause at the village green here; you'll see a pair of royal swans gliding regally in a little pool. The town is actually named after an early British officer, with the idea of swans apparently growing out of the name.

As you go south on U.S. Route 7 you'll see impressive views to left and right. The horizon is mountainous, with the Adirondacks to the west across Lake Champlain, while the Green Mountains rise to the east. Broad farmland is interspersed with rolling country.

Here and there a lone elm stands in the middle of a field,

apparently immune to the deadly Dutch elm disease. It is not a natural resistance that has saved it, however, but the lucky fact of its isolation. The bark beetle that carries the fungus is a weak flyer and can travel only about five hundred feet. After that the beetle falls to earth—and the tree has another year of reprieve.

Just north of St. Albans is a knoll where, in 1902, a lone wolf that had taken refuge in the area was killed. Peg and I have visited the spot, there in a little grove of trees on Aldis Hill. A stone has been set up to commemorate the event. As it turned out, this lone wolf was the last known member of its kind in all of Vermont.

South of St. Albans, Route 7 continues nearly ten miles to Georgia Center. After a large "S" turn, it makes its way past Arrowhead Mountain Lake.

A flooded valley of the Lamoille River, Arrowhead looks as if it could have been brought here from some northern wilderness. Stretches of dense forest line its shores. Canada geese drop down to its waters. Loons have been known to dive and swim and make the hills echo with the wildness of their laughter. You expect to see a moose wading along the shore—and, considering the present wanderings of this great creature, you just might not be disappointed.

Arrowhead Lake, actually held there by a dam, returns the Lamoille River to its course at the western edge of the town of Milton. Another large "S" turn takes Route 7 across the Lamoille and down through Chimney Corner (where you started after leaving I-89). The road wanders past more farmland and several small streams on its way to Colchester and back to Burlington.

Home again, you've traveled about three hours, more or less—maybe more, much more. After all, *somebody's* going to report seeing that mysterious Champ out there on the lake . . .

. . . *Or Find Out for Yourself*

"There are as many books about Vermont," say authors Christina Tree and Peter Jennison in their own book, "as there are about Maine." They point out you can get a list from the Vermont Historical Society, Montpelier, Vermont 05602. There's also a wealth of information at the Vermont Natural Resources Council, the Department of Forests and Parks, and the Fish and Wildlife Department—all in Montpelier.

Almost every town Information Center, plus State Welcome Centers at the borders, will have free copies of the Official State Highway Map. Get one for yourself, by all means.

You can also visit any of several pocket-sized segments of the Green Mountain State. I've already recommended the Fairbanks Museum in St. Johnsbury and the Merck Foundation Forest in Rupert. There's also the Green Mountain Audubon Center in Huntington with its library, museum, and special trail for the blind plus periodic nature programs.

One of my favorites is the Vermont Institute of Natural Science (VINS) in Woodstock. VINS has study specimens plus a large collection of colored slides and photographs. There are field trips, bird banding, and rehabilitation programs, an excellent raptor center for hawks and owls, and the popular ELF (Environmental Learning Facility) for schools.

In the line of books, perhaps you have a special interest in trees and shrubs, say, or birds. There are field guides for these and many other special subjects covering Vermont and adjoining regions. The following list represents but a few of the titles in the wealth of available books. Each deals specifically with Vermont and should help in your travels around the state.

Delorme, David, and Company. *The Vermont Atlas and Gazeteer.* Yarmouth, ME: David Delorme and Company, 1986. Vermont in five dozen detailed maps, plus sections listing museums, wildlife, campgrounds, more. Peg and I often drive with this large book spread open to the appropriate page as we go.

Ellison, Walter G. *A Guide to Bird Finding in Vermont.* Woodstock, VT: Vermont Institute of Natural Science, 1983. Where, how, and when to look for Vermont birds. Nancy Martin's maps and sketches add much to this easy-to-carry paperback: it's almost like a jaunt with one of New England's finest birders.

Johnson, Charles W. *Bogs of the Northeast.* Hanover, NH: University Press of New England, 1985. Abundantly illustrated. Bogs from Pennsylvania to Maine.

————. *The Nature of Vermont.* Hanover, NH: The University Press of New England, 1980. Vermont's State Naturalist takes us through the state's human, geologic, and natural history. Many photos, plus Jean Vissering's maps and Ann Pesiri's drawings.

Kunin, Madeleine, and Marilyn Stout. *The Big Green Book.* Barre, MA: Barre Publishing, 1976. A year-round guide, with drawings by Eleanor Hazard. Recreation, nature, arts and crafts, and—happily—things to do with children.

Lake Champlain Committee. *Exploring Lake Champlain and Its Highlands.* Burlington, VT: Lake Champlain Committee, 1981. A cooperative Vermont-New York venture. Where to fish, where to ride your bicycle—even first aid and the location of the nearest hospital. Profusely illustrated.

Lawrence, Gale. *The Beginning Naturalist.* Shelburne, VT: The New England Press, 1979. Week by week, through the year, you meet Vermont's plants and wildlife.

————. *A Field Guide to the Familiar.* Englewood Cliffs, NJ: Prentice-Hall, Inc., 1984. Tales of common Vermont plants and animals (squirrels, ragweed, toads, chickadees, and many more) serve as introductions to all their relatives. Illustrations by Adelaide Murphy.

————. *Vermont Life's Guide to Fall Foliage.* Montpelier, VT: Vermont Life Magazine, 1985.

Morrissey, Charles T. *Vermont: A History.* New York: W. W. Norton, 1981. This entertaining and informative volume in the *States and the Nation* series, by the former editor of *Vermont Life* magazine. Photographs by David Plowder. List of books for further reading.

Northern Cartographic, Inc. *The Vermont Road Atlas and Guide.* Burlington, VT: Northern Cartographic, Inc., 1985. Large enough to give good detail (9 X 12); maps with street names, guides to nature and recreation, more.

Scott, W. B. *Freshwater Fishes of Eastern Canada.* Toronto: University of Toronto Press, 1967. Fish know no national borders, so many Canadian species are Vermont fishes as well. Photos by W. H. Carrick.

Tree, Christina, and Peter Jennison. *Vermont: An Explorer's Guide.* Woodstock, VT: The Countryman Press, 1983. Area by area and town by town through the entire state. Natural areas, scenic drives, crafts. Richard Widhu's maps, plus many photographs.

Van Diver, Bradford, B. *Roadside Geology of Vermont and New Hampshire*. Missoula, MT: Mountain Press, 1987.

Vermont Life Magazine. *Vermont: A Special World*. Montpelier, VT: Vermont Life Magazine, 1969. Our Green Mountain State in words and photographs. A perennial favorite.

————. *Vermont for Every Season*. Montpelier, VT: Vermont Life Magazine, 1980. The many moods and faces of this most rural of all our fifty states. Richly illustrated with photographs.

Zarzynski, Joseph W. *Champ: Beyond the Legend*. Port Henry, NY: Bannister Publications, 1984. The search for the Lake Champlain monster. Illustrated with drawings and photographs.

THE END

Index

Abraham, Mount, 25, 36–40
Adder, checkered, 104
Addison, Vt., 173
Albany, Vt., 193
Alburg, Vt., 201
Alder, 40, 95, 96, 124, 189, 195, 201
Alfalfa, 11
Allen, Ethan, 200
Allen, Ira, 200
Amanita
  death angel, 63
  fly, 62–63
Amphibians, 75
Amphipod, 162
Anemone, 87
Ant, carpenter, 77
Aphid, 51, 116, 120
Appalachian Trail, 82, 86–89, 128
Apple
  fruit, 20, 129
  tree, 53
Arborvitae, 30
Arethusa, *see* orchid, bog pink
Arlington, Vt., 14, 16
Arrowhead, 154
Arrowhead Lake, 202
Asbestos, 27
Ascutney Train, 25
  See also erratic, glacial
Ash, 52, 87, 94
  American, 50, 84
  mountain, 32, 38
Asparagus, 18
Aspen, trembling, 95, 145
Aster, 87, 100–101

Balsam, Canada, 28
Barre, Vt., 27
Bass, black, 167

Bat, 121
Battell Trail, 36, 39–40
Bear, black, 51, 53, 65, 67, 80, 189; *illus.
  67*
  claw marks, *illus. 51*
Beaver, 84, 136, 144–45, 190, 201
  ponds, 131, 145, 192
Beech, 38, 50, 87, 88, 132, 190, 196;
  illus. 51
  nuts, 51
Beetle
  bark, 202
  diving, 163
  ground, 116
  ladybird, 116
  sexton, 138
  tiger, 116
  water penny, 134
  whirligig, 163
Bellows Falls, Vt., 130
Bennington, Vt., 14, 16
Birch, 50, 87, 132, 196
  gray, 40, 53, 95–96; *illus. 96*
  heartleaved, 32
  white (paper), 32, 38, 50, 88, 127, 190
  yellow, 50, 84, 88, 190, 191
Bittern, American, 172
Bittersweet, 97
Blackberry, 40, 93, 100
Blackbird, redwing, 109, 110, 179, 188;
  illus. 180
Black-eyed susan, 100
Black knot disease, 51
Bloodroot, 55
Bluebeads, 56, 87
Blueberry, 32, 39, 115, 124, 129
Bluebird, 108
Bluegill, 167
Boatman, water, 163

207

Bobcat, 68, 91; *illus. 92*
Bobolink, 112
Bolete, 62
Bowfin, 168
Bradford, Vt., 18
Brake, 99
Brandon, Vt., 44
Brattleboro, Vt., 128
Brighton State Park, 191
Bristleworm, 158
Bristol, Vt., 42, 71, 85
Brittleweed, 156
Brookfield, Vt., 43
Bryozoan, 157
Buckwheat, 18
Bullfrog, 169; *illus. 170*
Bullhead (bullpout), 167–68, 169
Bunchberry, 38, 54
Burdock, 10, 97, 132; *illus. 10*
Burlington, Vt., 183, 198
Bur-reed, 154
Butter-and-eggs, 9
Buttercup, 5, 7, 14, 137; *illus. 8*
Butterfly
  black swallowtail, 121
  blue satyr, 77
  cabbage, 121
  fritillary, silver-spangled, 121
  monarch, *illus. 121*
  mourning cloak, 77
  skipper, 121
  viceroy, 121
  white admiral, 121
Butternut, 50
Buttonbush, 198, 201

Cambridge, N.Y., 16
Cambridge, Vt., 46
Camel's Hump, 33
Canfield pines, 16
Cardinal, 110
Carp, 165–66, 200
Carrot, wild, *see* Queen Anne's lace
Caspian Lake, 195
Castleton, Vt., 85, 183
Catbird, 109
Caterpillar, tent, 77

Catfish, 167–68
Cattail, 153–54, 157, 181, 188, 195, 201;
  illus. 153
  swamp, 131
Cedar
  red, 29, 30, *illus. 31*
  white, 29–30, 192
Centipede, 79; *illus. 79*
Champ, *see* Lake Champlain Monster
Champlain, Lake 27, 157, 164, 165, 168,
  179, 183
Charlotte, Vt., 183, 184
Chelsea, Vt., 18
Cherry
  black, 38, 51–52, 88, 124, 190
  choke, 96
Chester, Vt., 131
Chestnut, water, 157
Chewink, *see* Towhee
Chickadee, 38, 72, 101, 108
Chicory, 14; *illus. 8*
Chimney Point, Vt., 42
Chipmunk, 35, 38, 53, 63, 67; *illus. 64*
Cicada, 120
Cinquefoil, 100
Clam, fingernail, 159
Clintonia, 38, 56, 87
Clover, 14, 97
  red, 10, *illus. 11*
  white, 10
Clubmoss, 58
Cockroach, 77–78
Colchester, Vt., 27, 183
Conch, 60
Concord, Vt., 189
Coneflower, 100–101
Copper, 27
Cornwall, Vt., 42, 85
Cowslip, 137
Coyote, eastern, 68, 70, 91
Craftsbury Common, Vt., 195
Cranberry, highbush, 132
Crayfish, 139, 160–61; *illus. 160*
Cricket
  field, 119
  snowy tree, 120
Crow, 34–35, 38, 110
Cyclops, 161

Dace, 134, 144, 168
Daddy longlegs, 117
Daisy, 5, 7, 14, 20, 101
Damselfly, 146–147, 162
Danby, Vt., 27
Dandelion, 5, 7, 20, 97; *illus. 6*
Danville, Vt., 188
Dead Creek Wildlife Refuge, 173, 179
Deer, 53, 66, 67, 84, 92, 96, 124, 126, 136, 189
Dewberry, 100
Discovery Museum, 47
Dock, common, 9
Dogwood
  dwarf, 54
  ground, 38
  panicled, 97–98
  red osier, 97
Dorset, Vt., 71, 127, 158
Dove, mourning, 111
Dover, Vt., 129
Dowsers' Convention, 188
Dragonfly, 115, 146–47, 162
Duck, 157, 198
  black, 146, 175
  bluebill, 176
  canvasback, 176
  dabbler, 174–75
  diving, 176
  fish (merganser), 176
  goldeneye, 176
  mallard, 175; *illus. 175*
  scaup, 176
  wood, 146, 175–76, 198; *illus. 177*
Duckweed, 157
Dummerston, Vt., 129
Dunmore, Lake, 139, 159
Dutch elm disease, 95, 202

Eagle, bald, 181
Eagle Bridge, N.Y., 17
Earthworm, 104, 158
Earwig, European, 117–19
East Brookfield, Vt., 43
East Calais, Vt., 186
East Middlebury, Vt., 42
East Montpelier, Vt., 186
East St. Johnsbury, Vt., 189

East Wallingford. Vt., 131
Eden, Lake, 195
Eden Mills, Vt., 195
Edge effect, 67
Eel, 164–65
  lamprey, 164, 169
Eelgrass, 156
Eft, red, *see* Salamander, red eft
Elm, American, 94–95, 112, 135, 201–2; *illus. 94*
Elmore, Lake, 197
Elodea, 156
Erratic, glacial, 25, 88, 192; *illus. 26*
Essex Jct., Vt., 46, 47
Evansville, Vt., 193

Fairbanks Museum, 188–89, 203
Fair Haven, Vt., 27
Falcon, peregrine, 193
Fern, 87
  bracken, 99, 124; *illus. 99*
  Christmas, 38, 40, 57–58, 131; *illus. 59*
  cinnamon, 57
  hay-scented (boulder), 57
  interrupted, 57; *illus. 58*
  ostrich, 136; *illus. 136*
  polypody, 88, 136
  sensitive, 99; *illus. 100*
Fiddleheads, 136–37
Fir
  balsam, 28, 38, 88, 124, 191
  Canada balsam, 28
Firefly, 121
Fireweed, 9
Fisher, Dorothy Canfield, 14
Fish ladder, 130
Flea, water, 161; *illus. 161*
Flicker, yellow-shafted, 107, 115; *illus. 108*
Fly
  black, 76, 142, 147
  caddis, 143; *illus. 143*
  carrion, 138
  crane, 164
  deer, 76
  stone, 142–43; *illus. 143*
Flycatcher, 115, 138
Fort Ticonderoga, N.Y., 42

Fox, 46, 97, 124
  red, 40, 68–70; *illus. 69*
Foxfire, 62
Foxville, Vt., 43
Frog, 104–5, 139
  green, 170
  leopard (common grass), 105
  spring peeper, 76, 105, 170
  tree, 105
  wood, 76
Fungus, bracket, 59; *illus. 60*

Gallup Mills, Vt., 190
Geese, behavior of, 157, 198
George D. Aiken Wilderness, 128
Gifford Woods State Park, 82, 86
Glochidia, 160
Glowworm, 121
Gnat, 116, 140, 146
Gneiss, 26
Goldenrod, 100–101
Goldfinch, 113
Goose
  Canada, 173–74, 202
  snow, 174
Goose Green, Vt., 18
Goshawk, 74
Grackle, common, 110
Granby, Vt., 190
Grand Isle, Vt., 200
Granite, 26–27
Graniteville, Vt., 43
Granville, Vt., 84
Granville Gulf Reservation, 84
Grape, 97, 98–99
Grass
  crab, 11
  orchard, 11
Grasshopper, 119–20; *illus. 119*
Green Mountain Audubon Center, 203
Green Mountain Club, 23, 38
Greensboro, Vt., 195
Grooves, glacial, 24; *illus. 24*
Grosbeak, 32
Grouse, ruffed, 38, 54, 70–71; *illus. 71*
Guildhall, Vt., 190
Gull

greater black-backed, 178
herring, 178; *illus. 178*
ringbilled, 114, 178, 186; *illus. 114*
Hancock, Vt., 44, 84
Hardhack, 52–53
  bush, 94
Hardwick, Vt., 188, 195
Hare, snowshoe, 65, 66, 124; *illus. 66*
Harrier, northern, 179
Harvestmen, 117
Hawk
  fish, 180, 200
  marsh, 179, 181
  red-tail, 109; *illus. 109*
  sparrow (kestrel), 107
Hawkweed, 5
Hellebore, false (Indian Poke), 137–38
Hemlock, 28–29, 88, 135; *illus. 29, 31*
Hepatica, 55
Heron
  black-crowned night, 172
  great blue, 131, 172, 198; *illus. 173*
  little green, 146
Hickory, shagbark, 52
Hirudin, 158
Hobblebush, *see* Witch hobble
Hornbeam, hop, 53
Hornet
  horse guard, 116
  white-faced, 116
Horsetail, 155–56; *illus. 156*
Hummingbird, 57
Hyde Park, Vt., 195, 197

Ironwood, 52
Ivy
  five-leaved, 98
  poison, 97, 102; *illus. 103*
  scarlet, 98

Jack-in-the-pulpit, 37, 56
Jamaica, Vt., 162
Jasper, 27
Jay
  blue, 35, 88, 110–11; *illus. 111*
  gray, 189
Jay, Vt., 196

Jeffersonville, Vt., 44, 46
Johnson, Vt., 27, 46, 197
Junco, 38
Juniper, 30

Kestrel, 107
Killdeer, 114–15; *illus. 115*
Kingbird, 110
Kingfisher, belted, 139
Knapweed, 14
Knight Point State Park, 200

Ladybug, 116
Ladyslipper
  pink, 56
  yellow, 150
Lady's tresses, 151; *illus. 151*
Lake Champlain Monster, 183–85
Lake Elmore State Park, 193, 197
Lake St. Catherine State Park, 126
Larch, 31
Lark, horned, 114
Larrabee's Point, Vt., 42
Leafhopper, 120
Leech, 158; *illus. 158*
Lichen, 57, 88
Lightning bug, 121
Lilac, 12
Lily
  day, 9
  pond
    white, 155
    yellow, 154–55; *illus. 155*
  trout, 56, 87
Limestone, 27
Lincoln, Vt., 25, 36–40, 42
Liverwort, 87, 135; *illus. 135*
Locust (cicada), 120
Londonderry, Vt., 90
Long Trail, 23, 36–40, 82, 128
Loon, common, 172, 202; *illus. 174*
Loosestrife (Long Purples), 16
Lord's Prayer Rock, 42
Lowell, Vt., 27, 195
Ludlow, Vt., 131, 137

Maidstone State Park, 191
Manchester, Vt., 126

Manchester Center, Vt., 89, 90, 127
Mansfield, Mount, 33, 46
Mantis, praying, 116; *illus. 117*
Maple, 38, 94, 131, 132, 196
  red, 49, 96, 135, 149, 189, 201; *illus.
    49*
  striped, 38
  sugar, 48–49, 53, 84, 87–88, 96, 124,
    127, 188, 195; *illus. 49*
Marble, 27
Marigold, marsh, 137
Martin, purple, 179
Mayfly, 141–42; *illus. 142*
Mayweed, 7–8
Meadowlark, 112
Meadowsweet, 94
Mendon, Vt., 82
Merck Foundation, 127, 203
Merganser, 176
Mice, *see* Mouse
Middlebury, Vt., 42, 85
Middletown Springs, Vt., 133
Midge, 164; *illus. 165*
Milfoil, European, 101, 157, 200
Milkweed, 101
Millipede, 79–80; *illus. 80*
Mink, 124, 139
Minnow, 168
Missisquoi National Wildlife Refuge 174,
    179, 201
Mite, 78, 117
  water, 164; *illus. 165*
Moccasin
  flower, 56
  water, 172
Mockingbird, 109, 110
Mold, Fred, 190
Mole, 122
Montgomery Center, Vt., 196
Montpelier, Vt., 186, 203
Moose, 124, 131, 189, 190, 202
Morrisville, Vt., 46, 195, 197
Mosquito, 76, 163–64
Moss, 56–57, 87, 135
  animal, 157–58
  haircap, 57
  reindeer, 57
  sphagnum, 147

211

Moss Glen Falls, 44, 84
Moth
  gypsy, 77
  spotted forester, 77
Mountain ash, 32, 38
Mouse, 34, 104, 136
  deer, 64; *illus. 65*
  meadow, 92
  white-footed, 38
Mud Creek Waterfowl Area, 201
Mullein (flannel plant), 9
Mushroom, 59–63
  amanita, *see* Amanita
  ink cap, 62
  Jack-o-lantern, 62
  oyster, 62; *illus. 62*
  puffball, 60–62; *illus. 61*
Muskellunge, 168
Muskrat, 131, 157, 181, 183, 190, 198
  house 181, 183
Mussel, freshwater, 159, 181, 198
Mustard, wild, 100
Myriophyllum, *see* Milfoil, European

Nettle, 37
Newport, Vt., 193
Newt, 75
Northfield, Vt., 43
North Hero, Vt., 200–201
No-see-ums, 76, 164
Nuthatch, white, 72

Oak, 52, 53
  poison, 102; *illus. 103*
  red, 52
  white, 52
Old Man's Beard, 32–33, 39; *illus. 33*
Oppossum, Virginia, 102–3
Orchid
  bog pink, 149–50, 190
  ladyslipper, 56
Orchis, yellow fringed , 150
Oriole, northern, 112–13; *illus. 113*
Orleans, Vt., 193
Osprey, 180–81, 200; *illus. 182*
Otter, 139; *illus. 140*

Owl
  barred, 131; *illus. 132*
  great horned, 74
Oxalis, *see* Sorrel, wood

Paintbrush, devil's, 5
Panton, Vt., 71
Partridge, 70
Pawlet, Vt., 126–27
Peeper, spring, 105
Perch, yellow, 167; *illus. 167*
Peru, Vt., 158
Pheasant, ring-necked, 112
Phoebe, eastern, 138
Pickerel, 166
Pickerel weed, 154
Pigeon, 193
Pike
  northern, 166
  walleyed, 166
Pine
  beach, 155–56
  needles, *illus. 31*
  Norway, 30
  red, 30, 195
  running (clubmoss), 58
  white, 16, 30, 89, 189, 190, 197
Pineapple weed, 7
Pitcher Plant, 148; *illus. 149*
Pittsfield, Vt., 84
Poison ivy, *see* Ivy, poison
Pogonia, rose, 150
Poke, Indian, 138
Pompanoosuc, Vt., 18
Pondweed, 156, 157
Poplar, 40, 53, 94, 131, 135
Popple (Aspen), 95, 145
Porcupine, 35, 38, 46, 64, 84, 136, 196
Poultney, Vt., 27, 126
Pout, horned, 167–68
Pownal, Vt., 14
Primrose, 20
Proctor, Vt., 27
Puffball, 60–62; *illus. 61*
Pumpkinseed, 167
Punkies, 76, 164
Putney, Vt., 129

Quartz, 38, 43, 88
Queen Anne's lace, 17, 101; *illus. 17*

Rabbit, cottontail, 65–66, 93; *illus. 93*
Raccoon, 68, 97, 139–40
  paw print, *illus. 141*
Ragweed, 10
Raspberry, 93, 100, 129
Rattlesnake, timber, 74, 104; *illus. 105*
Raven, 34–35, 38, 128
Rawsonville, Vt., 90
Redstart, 113
Reef, coral, 183
Ripton, Vt., 44, 123
Robert Frost Interpretive Trail, 123–24
Robin, 109, 139
  ground, *see* Towhee
Rochester, Vt., 84
Rock tripe, 88
Rockwell, Norman, 14
Rose, wild, 100
Roxbury, Vt., 43
Rupert, Vt., 71, 127
Rushes, 201
  scouring, 155
Rutland, Vt., 82, 85
Ryegrass, 11

St. Albans, Vt., 202
St. Johnsbury, Vt., 188–89
Salamander
  brook, 75
  pond, 75, 170
  red-backed, 75
  red eft, 75, 106
  spotted, 75–76
Salmon, 144, 165, 169
  landlocked, 165, 191; *illus. 166*
Sand Bar State Park, 198
Sandpiper, 179
  solitary, 139
  spotted, 145–46
Sapsucker, yellow-bellied, 72; *illus. 73*
Schist, 25, 43
Scud, 162
Sculpin, brook, 144
Sedge, 33, 147, 148
  cotton, 148

Shadbush, 38
Shale, 27
Sheepshead, 168
Sherburne, Vt., 82
Sherburne Pass, 22, 82, 86, 88
Shiner, 145
Shoreham, Vt., 42
Shrew, 34, 70; *illus. 34*
  water, 140
Shrewsbury, Vt., 131
Shrike, northern, 109–10
Skunk, 46, 68, 74
Skunk cabbage, 137–38; *illus. 138*
Slate, 27, 126
Slug, 80, 81
Smartweed, water, 156
Smelt, 168–69
Smugglers Notch, 44, 46
Snail, 80, 81
  pond, 158
  ram's horn, 146
  tadpole, 146
  white-lipped, 80; *illus. 81*
Snake
  black rat, 104
  garter, 104
  green, 104
  horsehair, 146; *illus. 146*
  little brown, 74
  milk, 104
  red-bellied, 74
  ringneck, 74
  timber rattle, 74, 104; *illus. 105*
  water, 171–72
Sorrel, wood, 40, 55; *illus. 55*
South Alburg, Vt., 201
South Corinth, Vt., 18
South Hero, Vt., 200
South Lincoln, Vt., 169
South Londonderry, Vt., 90
South Newfane, Vt., 129
South Northfield, Vt., 43
South Royalton, Vt., 20
Sowbug, 161
Sparrow, 72
  song, 113
  white-throated, 38
Spatterdock, 154–55; *illus. 155*

Spider
  diving, 164
  funnel-web, 117
  northern garden, 116; *illus. 118*
  weaver, 117
  wolf, 78–79, 117
Spring beauty, 55–56
Spruce, 28, 191
  black, 149
  red, 28, 38, 88
Squirrel, 52, 53, 63, 136
  flying, 63
  gray, 63
  red, 38, 63, 88
Starling, 107
Steeplebush, 94
Stockbridge, Vt., 84
Stowe, Vt., 46
Strafford, Vt., 27
Strawberry, 100, 129
Sturgeon, 168, 183
Sumac, 96, 131, 132
  poison, 101–2; *illus 103*
  staghorn, 101–2; *illus. 102*
Sundew, 148; *illus. 150*
Sunfish, 167
Swallow
  bank, 124, 130
  barn, 146
  tree, 108
Swallowtail, tiger, 120
Swan, royal, 201
Swanton, Vt., 171, 174, 201

Tadpole, 106
Talc, 27
Tamarack (larch), 30, 31
Teal
  bluewinged, 175
  greenwinged, 175
Termite, 76
Tern
  black, 179
  common, 179
Thetford, Vt., 27
Thistle, 9
Thrasher, brown, 109

Thrush, 113
  hermit, 72, 74
Tick, 78
Timothy, 11
Tinmouth Channel Wildlife Management
  Area, 132
Titmouse, tufted, 110
Toad
  American, 105, 170; *illus. 106*
  tree, 170
Touch-me-not, 37
Towhee, chestnut-sided, 112
Trefoil, birdsfoot, 11, 12
Trillium
  red, 37, 56
  painted, 56
Trout, 127, 134, 141
  brook, 87, 143–44, 145, 165
  brown, 143–44, 165
  furbearing, 193
  lake, 165, 191
  rainbow, 165, 193
Troy, Vt., 196
Tunbridge, Vt., 18
Turkey, wild, 71, 112, 124, 126
Turtle
  painted, 171
  snapping, 171; *illus. 171*
  wood, 75

Vallisneria (eelgrass), 156
Vermont Institute of Natural Science
  (VINS), 203
"Vernal pools," 106
Vershire, Vt., 27
Vetch, 9
Victory, Vt., 189
Victory Bog, 190
Violet, 87
  dogtooth, 56
  yellow, 37
Vireos, olive-and-white, 72
Virginia creeper, 98
Vole, meadow, 92
Vulture, turkey, 110, 181

Walden, Vt., 188
Walleye, 166

Wallingford, Vt., 27, 131
Warblers, 72, 115
  yellow-throated, 138
Warren, Vt., 36, 43
Wasp, 116
Waterbug, giant, 162; *illus. 162*
Waterbury, Vt., 46
Water-hopper, 161
Water penny, 134
Water strider, 140–41
Waxwing, cedar, 115
Weasel, 68, 124
Websterville, Vt., 43
Westminster, Vt., 130
Westmore, Vt., 192
White River Jct., Vt., 18, 20
Whiting, Vt., 85
Wildcat (bobcat), 68
Williamstown, Vt., 43
Williamsville, Vt., 129
Willoughby, Lake, 192–93
Willow, 53, 94, 149, 190, 195, 201
Wilmington, Vt., 129

Windflower, 87
Windsor, Vt., 25
Witch hazel, 135
Witch Hobble, 38, 53–54; *illus. 54*
Wolcott, Vt., 195
Wolf, 202
Woodbine, 98, 131
Woodbury, Vt., 188
Woodchuck, 40, 97; *illus. 98*
Worcester, Vt., 197
Woodcock, 139
Woodpecker, 101, 107, 115
  downy, 72
  hairy, 72
  pileated, 72; *illus. 73*
Wood roach, 77–78
Worm
  Gordian, 146
  measuring, 77
Wren, house, 108–9
Wrightsville Dam Recreation Area, 197

Yarrow, 101